Tony Curtis

FROM THE FORTUNATE ISLES:
NEW & SELECTED POEMS

Tony Curtis

FROM THE FORTUNATE ISLES:
NEW & SELECTED POEMS

Seren is the book imprint of
Poetry Wales Press Ltd.
57 Nolton Street, Bridgend, Wales, CF31 3AE
www.serenbooks.com
facebook.com/SerenBooks
twitter@SerenBooks

The right of Tony Curtis to be identified as
the author of this work has been asserted in accordance
with the Copyright, Designs and Patents Act, 1988.

ISBN: 978-1-78172-330-2
E-book: 978-1-78172-335-7
Kindle: 978-1-78172-336-4

A CIP record for this title is available from the British Library.

The publisher acknowledges the financial assistance of the Welsh Books Council.

Cover Artwork: Mandela Poterion II by Alan Salisbury
Oil on board, courtesy the Artist.
The Arches collages, courtesy of John Digby

Printed by TJ International, Cornwall.

Author Website: www.tonycurtispoet.com

Contents

WAR VOICES (1995)

THE ARCHES (1998)
With collages by John Digby

HEAVEN'S GATE (2001)

Introduction

I began to write poetry with serious intent in my first year at Swansea University in the 1965/66 academic year, so this collection of my poems covers fifty years. Selecting from such a long period has been challenging, but I hope that the final section in this book of uncollected poems, my tenth collection, "From the Fortunate Isles" suggests that in my seventh decade what I have to say and the poetry which chooses to say it remains strong and vibrant.

The poet who most impressed me as a guest at university was Dannie Abse whose reading in 1967 was inspiring by virtue of the poems themselves and the way that they were read. Dannie became a friend and a mentor for over thirty years. In my earlier years Roland Mathias and John Tripp, as well as tutors at Goddard College in Vermont were supportive readers. My colleagues at my university provided a sympathetic context for personal writing over a number of years. Also, friends in the visual arts have inspired ideas and have been generous in collaborating on poetry projects. It is fitting that an Alan Salisbury painting should appear on the cover of this book, some thirty years after his work was on the cover of my *Selected Poems 1970-1985*, published by Poetry Wales Press, which became Seren: the support of staff at the press, especially Mick Felton, have been crucial to my career as a poet, as a critic of art and literature and of my prose works. For the last four years in the Gelligaer, Alchemy of Water and Aberfan Voices projects Grahame Davies has brought his Welsh poetry to work on our shared vision of Wales.

My first reader, proof reader and listener from 1965 has been my wife, Margaret. This affirmative taking of stock is for her, my son Gareth, my daughter Bronwen and the next generation – Megan, Ellis, Huw, Tomos and Kate.

Tony Curtis

Snapshot: Man And Bird

He poses for me at the back of the shed,
hand stretched out confidently to hold
the old bird first back from Nantes.
This pigeon bounces jerkily to the invitation,
perches knowingly on the hand.
In the left corner of the viewfinder is the loft,
green and white stripes freshly painted.
If I open my left eye the camera squint blurs
and is over-ridden by the widening garden:
potatoes flowering, a line of crisping clothes,
a ragged towel holed, through which the sky shows:
these have nothing to do with the photograph.
In the print they will no more appear than
the plump corn the pigeon kisses in his hand.

The Mystery of the Homing Pigeon

for Blundell & Son, N.W.P.F.

The mystery of the homing pigeon
is being cracked.
A professor at Cornell tracks
the birds in his twin-engined Comanche,
asserts the dependence on sun and moon,
what ancient mariners they make;
whilst a computer at the Max Planck Institute
simulates wind, magnetic field and flight.
When I tell you, you say you don't care:
"Good lofts make good birds",
receive the applause of their wings
as they take the air.

Travelling

Leaving Croesgoch, the night closes in
locking the land firm
as we drive southward home.

Past Solva, and the tight twists
of the road spiral us towards sea.

Newgale strung by phosphorescent surf,
windsong and the slush of pebbles:
rain rinsing through our headlights' mist.

Six months from this Boxing Day
and our limousine inching
away from clustered scrapers,
down the cloudbursted freeway
over the Hudson to Kennedy:
a grounded flight,
the banal limbo of a terminal wait.

Hung like waves between two points,
all our time we are travelling,
unwinding the road home,
the wipers an insistent metronome,

eyes cutting into the night
needing water and light,
water and light.

Killing Whales

Eye sharpening down the line of the cannon:
The crack of the shot
                              high whine
Aching seconds of rope
Spiralling out of the basket.

Slack rope
                  and the second, muffled explosion
Tears through bone and blubber.

Whale-back island rising from the deep.
Blow-hole like steam from a boiler.
Wild plunging
                  then rising
Resigned to the ship's tether.

Belly over in a slow-motion twist
That could be the discomfort of an itch;
Until that last, low spouting
Like brown water draining a rusty cistern.

Grapple, winch the carcass up the slope:
Out of its element the mass is grotesque.

                  Slice
Through the blubber to the red, hot meat.

In the ship's belly white flashes
Pattern the darkness of a sonar screen.

Circling the fleet, whales sing deeply
Love to the hulls of factory ships.

Two Images From Dreams

One.

A house across the street;
bedroom window open to view
and a woman lying on a large bed,
her head crooked back to the window.
She is old: white hair matted like wool
over the pillow.
                    Below, out of focus,
the street busies itself.
The bedroom door opens,
a man enters, dressed formally.
His face is two faces:
                         one
is a moustachioed villain of Melodrama
curling a murderous smile;
the other a mourner.
His hand carries a wreath of poppies
finished with a blood-red rose at the centre.

Pause.

The woman moves:
                    her hand
stretches to the flowers
and with the weight of her whole body's arch
pulls the rose away,
falling back to the bed,
arm out rigidly over the window ledge.
Her hand, enormous, opens like a spring trap.
The rose balances at the height,
thorn hooked to the palm;
slowly, loose petals detach themselves
and fall, like drops of blood,
to the street.

Two.

A man is locking the large, heavy door
of a high-roofed hall.
An impression of neatness:
he is, possibly, an attendant, curator.
The centre of the door, at the point
where its diagonal bars cross,
dissolves into a camera-hole
through which I pass.
Inside, the skeletons of prehistoric beasts
loom hugely on spindle-legs.
Shadows move in abstract on the back wall,
and caged in the ribs of a dinosaur
a bird flutters wildly,
cutting and flapping at the bars
of the ancient guts.
A man is locking the large, heavy door
of a high-roofed hall:
an impression of neatness.

Family of Saltimbanques, Paris 1905

Six figures in a line
Posed against a blue-yellow desert.
They are caught in the middle of nowhere,
In the middle of living.

There is a strong fatman
Ridiculous with his red outfit and crooked hat.

There are two boys,
One holding a barrel, empty as a lost dream,
The other fingering a red scarf
Which is slipping off his shoulder
Like the past.

Harlequin is a strong father,
Clown statesman defying the indifferent desert
Holding, protecting
His daughter, who has eyes only
For her basket of pale flowers.

The last figure
Is a calmly beautiful woman
Posing like a rose behind glass.
She sits near a pitcher of water
And has never been to the desert.

In Camera

At the moment when
lights stretch and stab
in a blinding sear,
the glass is an instant frost,
flash-back to crusted window
holding all the snow-filled mornings;

at the moment when
the shoulder cracks,
ball spinning out of your grasp,
distant touchline shouts;

at the sad last moment
by the bed huge with grief,
shoes snap through gravel,
trees stirred by wind;

at the point when
your face bites unheard
shouts into the pillow
past her quickening

yes yes yes yes

hair wet in your mouth

behind you
always behind you
the camera turns
whirrs to an image
                    and
yes
it is your hand on the megaphone
trumpeting directions,

you cut and splice
concerned with the composition
of the scene

Preparations

In the valley there is an order to these things:
Chapel suits and the morning shift called off.
She takes the bus to Pontypridd to buy black,
But the men alone proceed to the grave,
Neighbours, his butties, and the funeral regulars.
The women are left in the house; they bustle
Around the widow with a hushed, furious
Energy that keeps grief out of the hour.

She holds to the kitchen, concerned with sandwiches.
It is a ham-bone big as a man's arm and the meat
Folds over richly from her knife. A daughter sits
Watching butter swim in its dish before the fire.
The best china laid precisely across the new tablecloth:
They wait. They count the places over and over like a rosary.

Strongman

A strongman you say.
Home from work would stretch his arms
and hang his five sons from them
turning like a roundabout.
A carpenter who could punch nails
into wood with a clenched fist,
chest like a barrel with a neck
that was like holding onto a tree.

In the final hour
your hands between the sheets
to lift him to the lavatory
slipped under a frame of bones like plywood.
No trouble – he said. No trouble, Dad –
you said. And he died in the cradle of your arms.

From Vermont

The snow breathes and stretches the length of the tall pines.
From dawn, each second of the sun,
bunched snow wrinkles and creases, its layers
tightening around the needles and branches
until the grip closes firm on itself and the load falls free.

The trees moan inside their snow
(low like the other's dreams after love)
though there is no movement, there is no wind,
nothing to stir the sharp air but walking,
the lungs' steady pump.

Tonight when I phone the line blurs,
marking the distance between us.
You'll be in our bed before my meal is finished.
When I tell you I'm missing you,
that I need you, you smile – "I bet."

Love, listen, we are so far
along the way of one another
the hold is firm enough, warm inside cold,
and when it falls it's still wrapped
around our joined shape.

Swimming Class

Our children are learning to save themselves.
From the pool, his shouts, their splashing and cries:
frog-legs, dog-paddle, flop-dives –
they ride the water, held by our breath.
We've wrapped their modest cocks with towels,
tousled and talced them dry, cowled like monks.
Pulling the wet valves, the stale air farts out:
the floaters squash like rotten fruit.

When we have gone the instructor's smoke hangs
over the tiles. He watches his butt sizzle
in a stream of piss, wipes off the mirror's dew
and inflates his biceps and chest. Every week we push
them further to a length. The world beyond
is made by accidents. We love them and they could drown.

Pwllcrochan

I spent weeks down here:
Spring and Autumn planting and picking,
thick wedges of bread and tea,
hands smelling of earth and potato juice;
story-book childhood weekends of stolen
apples, blown birds' eggs, trespassing;
rainy evenings exploring the smugglers' cellar,
shadows jerked alive by the throbbing light generator.

The Old Rectory has gone –
scraped flat for a Texaco car-park,
abandoned after six months.
Now, outbuildings enclose a grassy space,
an ache of absence.
Down the rutted lane to the bay:
from the narrow, stone bridge inland
the refinery spreads its shining tentacles,
its waste-burner roaring, glowing through the day.

The small bay is thick with reeds, wiry grass:
stream trickling over Wellington-hungry mud
to slide beneath shells and sandstone shale
into the once-secret Haven.
Across the deep water from our fishing rocks
the gantries suckle from fat tankers,
steel arteries pulse away through the hills.

Looking back up to the road
I frame you in the camera lens,
centred by the cleft of the sloping fields.
You turn, Gareth smiles in your arms
and the photo worked perfectly,
bringing you into focus
and leaving all the rest behind.

As we walk back to the car, stepping from
bank to tussock, the marks of our weight in the mud stay,
draw an ooze of oil to rainbow our way.

Letter from John

It was not for want of think
that I did not rite you a love letter sooner
and this cause I think of you every hour of the day
and every day of the year
and I do love your father to cause he did lend you the horse
and cart to brought me to the train on Monday.
I shall never forget to remember what you did tell
me when coming in the cart. Oh! Mary Jane
stick to your promise won't you my dear.

I did rive Pontyprydd safe and sound
and I did go strait to the Shop
and when the master did see me he did say
"Man from where are you?"
And I told him that I was John from Maenclochog
coming to work in his shop. Then he nowed me in a minit.

Look you my work is selling cotten
and tapes and hundreds of other things.
They do all call it Happy Compartment
or something, but indeed to goodness
it was not very happy at all to be here without you,
the girl I do love better than nobody
(for all the time I am thinking of you)

Oh, yes you will ask my mother to send my watch
if it is working
cause it will be very handy for me in the morning
to know what o'clock it is.
She do know my directions.

There is a lot of girls in this shop
but not one to match you Mary Jane.
How long you are going to stop

in Mrs. Jones' again, Mary Jane,
cause I will try and get you a job at Pontyprydd
to be a Millander.
I will hask Mr. Thomas the draper about a position for you
for they say he do give very good vittels to his clerks.
It will be better by half for you to come
to Pontyprydd cause then we will be near to one another
for the forehead of Mrs. Thomas' shop
and the forehead of our shop
be quite close to one another
and by and by we will marry
is it not my dear?

They say that shop girls do not make good wifes
but you know what Mr. Evans the schoolmaster said:
"Put a nose wherever you like
and it will be a nose
and put a donkey wherever you like
and it will be a donkey."
And like that you are Mary my dear.
I believe shop girls will make good wifes
if they have a chance.

Well, I will not rite you a bigger this time
for if it was twice bigger I could never
tell you how I love you.

I send you a piece of Poultry
I did make last night
and if you have not received it
send back at once.

Letter from John – This poem was "found" in one of only two letters in my grand-
mother's house in Carmarthen. She was Beatrice Mary Curtis.

I must finish cause I can hear somebody
asking for hooks and eyes
and your loving John must go forward

Oh Mary Jane my darling
I love you in my heart
I told you so last monday
When coming in the cart

Suppose the horse did understand
What I to you did say
I have no doubt my darling
It would have runned away.

I'll always love you Mary Jane
And you be true to me
Come up soon to Pontyprydd
To sell some Drapery.

My Father

My father is a shadow
growing from my feet.

This shadow grows from one minute
past the noon of my life
and trails me like water.

My father is mending all fifty-three of his cars.
He works in a garden shed
by the caged light of an inspection lamp.
The red glow at his lips shows constantly
small and fierce like an airliner overhead
or the startled eye of a fox.

Ash falls onto the greased parts
of the dynamo.
He hawks and spits through the door.

His hands and nails black with grease
come out from the old paint tin
he has filled with petrol.
Like rare birds they rise
their plumage glistening and sharp
spilling green and blue and silver.

Those hands that my forehead meets
briefly and shivering.
Those rough hands I run from
like the borders of a strange country.

Poem From My Father

The two who spotted her
– approaching but no closer –
come back up the beach like dogs from the waves.

I never thought you squeamish of flesh,
and though your life has been frayed and tattered
by your predilictions for the wrong choice,

you take on the indisputable fact of death,
dealing with the mess, putting on responsibility like a coat;
your second casual corpse in as many months.

She has fed the fishes
her face.
The rings of her fingers have slipped their flesh.

Belly pregnant with the blue swell of her guts.
They have sucked through her breasts
to the heart's cage.

Six weeks adrift the wrong side of living,
she is something quite other
than wife, young woman, mother.

There's an old blanket you drop over her,
a stone laid at each corner.
Sand could open and swallow her spread body's horror.

Sentry for an hour before the police,
your seventh cigarette beginning to taste;
smoke against a sky tight as a drum.

The sea offers up ourselves to ourselves.
Looking out to the grey island,
you start to hum.

My Father in Pembrokeshire

One of those godly days on the Headland,
gorse with the yellow coming to burst,
the tight heather and curled grasses sprung underfoot.

Such days are numbered for you,
we spend our time here like wages.
Precious the slow, awkward breathing,
the laboured talk is precious.

The sand over on Caldey never seemed so bright,
the island stretching empty arms to the west
in that early summer Sunday
before the trade fills the streets and the beaches,
and the noise of the day washes
out from the town a mile or more,
louder than sea.

I have to go further down.
I have to go down to the water.
The way is worn rough and safe;
I crawl to the edge of a chimney shaft.
The sea lies calm as well-water,
green with rocks growing patterns underneath.

To lose myself in the long moment,
drinking in the depth, the abstract shapes.

Back at the top, you say –
Feel my neck –
and the growths blossom along your throat
under my fingers.

Under the sun, the prodigal sky,
there are no healing waters.

To My Father

Bellringing was another
of the things you didn't teach me.

How many crooked ladders did we climb?
How many belfries did we crouch in?
The musty smell of the years in the wood beams,
the giant domes balanced to move
against a man's pull.
Stories of jammed trapdoors and madness
in the deafening that draws blood.
Once you rang for the Queen
and I watched
all that pomp ooze into the cold stone of the cathedral.

I wanted to take the smooth grip of a rope
and lean my weight into it.
I wanted timing.
I wanted you to teach me
to teach my son's son.

Turning your back on that
brings our line down. What
have you left me? What sense
of the past? I could have lost myself in the mosaic
of Grandsires, Trebles and Bobs,
moved to that clipped calling of the changes.

I know now the churchbells' coming over the folded
town's Sunday sleep carries me close to tears,
the noise of worship and weddings and death
rolling out
filling the hollow of my throat.

Return to the Headland

There seems no point in angels
or ogres. Now I have no need
for the cartoons of guilt or shame.
The dead go where we send them.
At the crematorium I read 'Do Not Go Gentle'
before the vicar's book freed
your soul or whatever it be that soars
from the husk of flesh.
The curtains purred to their close.
Outside, the long summer of rain,
grey and grey and grey blurred
over Narberth's sodden hills.

It would be easy to construct a myth.
The box jammed under
the baby-seat in the back of the car,
bumping our way up to the Headland.
Early evening. The sea green and flat,
moving and murmuring in the hollows beneath
our feet. Not a cloud shaped, though the horizon
cast across Wales is dimming into grey.
The urn is some sort of alloy
like a child's toy, light and wrapped around
what we're told are your ashes.

Not in the sea – says my mother –
he was never a man for the sea –
I step off the path to the slope of rocks
and two rabbits break for cover
from the startled grass.
The stuff shakes out and falls free:
dust, ash on the stones, my shoes.
Stiff-armed, I send the empty tin
over the edge right down to the water.

A jet chalks its line high above the ocean,
pushing steadily away from night.
We turn our backs on a sky that goes on for ever.

Poem for John Tripp

We have filled this church, like a cold, damp barn
perched above Lancashire mills on the edge of the moors.
Wind that razors through to the bones;
leavings of snow on the hills,
moulded to the underside of low stone walls.

With god-knows what light, the pre-Raphaelite
stained glass records the Whitworth's son and wife:
In Loving Memory – 27 years – 31 years. 1894.
Today is Barbara in her box,
chrysanthemums, the death flowers, arranged on the lid.

Our third funeral within a year –
this friend dead at thirty-two,
her daughters too young to know what it is they feel,
like an unseen draught chilling their dreams.
I've had enough of this coldness, of loss.

John, we are under the weight of this thing
And we wol sleen this false traytour Deeth
clench the fist around the pen, we riotoures three:
you and I and the third – our dead friends and fathers,
on the road, at the desk, looking over our shoulders.

The Weather Vane

The wind is rising:
the plastic man turns his handle
and the paddles go over and over.
A trick of the eye.
The paddles turn the man,
the wind animates him.

An evening in September: light
blue and brown streaking the West sky.
The vane's tail-fin catches and spins
the whole thing on its pivot.
So the man bends and works, spins
to hold in the trough of the wind.
Dad, it was you painted the post
and fixed it firm. Last year.
That same wind moves your ashes tonight in the sea
and the grass in Pembrokeshire.

In the Summer I saw the whole stretch of our coast
from thirty-five thousand feet.
Flat Holm to Pennar and not a cloud.
South Wales spread out like a school atlas,
so green and small before the hours of ocean.
It was like looking back on our lives.

The last light's fallen away.
There's no man or paddles or wishing well.
You and I separated now by a long year,
going our ways into the second winter.

Letting Go

The trees shake their snow
like a dog at your window.

The world is plant and animal –
it melts, it dies, it falls.

So we make of it art.
Those dry brown grasses in the snow:

the summer's Queen Anne's lace,
old women laying their bones against white sheets.

That gust of wind, the hand
lifts snow dust from the pines.

It powders across the field, turns to
breath in the air. Something to do

with letting go.

Tannenbaum

Wooden strawberries, tinsel pythons,
plastic icicles with shepherd's crook hooks,
the toilet roll angel from school
– we amass the stuff of celebration.

I screw the tree
hard into its base and each
turn skews it further from the true
upright. Year by year

we dress the tree, finger
the strings of lights,
touching every brittle stamen,
telling the rosary of the snapped elements.

It never works, never the first time.
There's always something loose,
something to curse at.
A star falls, needles rain onto the carpet.

In the late Summer the children
discover its skeleton in the hedge.
On our bonfire it crackles and spits,
breaks down to a snowy white ash.

Staring into the flames
I think of Christmas,
my mother visiting us,
using my study as her bedroom.

On my desk she lays a bracelet,
three rings, a watch and the pendant
that holds my father's face.
Gold, silver, all the things that melt.

Crane-flies

for Gareth

The foghorns keening in the bay
belie these sultry days.
September's Indian Summer:
our apple-tree's grown sweeter than ever,
hazelnuts ripen and brown,
there's a morning haze across the lawn.

This year so many crane-flies
– Daddy-long-legs –
each room in our house has a pair.
They whirr and tick, crucify
themselves in high corners, against lamps.

Yesterday you came from school hurt
that boys were pulling wings apart,
snapping flies' legs like twigs
until you threatened them with worse.
"Crane-flies," you told me,
"the proper name is crane-flies."
Your anger was wonderful,
I could have squeezed you till you cried.

All the week the tv has brought us
the Phalange massacres in Beirut –
mangled corpses parcelled in sheets.
"Goyim murders goyim, and they hang the Jew!"
Words, gunfire: the tangled lies of hate:
this will be called The September Slaughter.
It will blur into Middle East History.
I would not expect you to distinguish it
from all the other crimes even if you should
some day read it in a book.

The Infants' Christmas Concert

A moment of hush, held breath –
the fairies and robbers, the soldiers
and dancers are in position
– then the piano begins.
This sounds otherworldly,
each note a drop of water falling distantly.

Angels swallow trumpets,
a robot trips and turtles in his cardboard shell;
the ballerina crumples and cries.
They may not know why, but still
perform for us the pattern of sentiment,
superstition and love: we sigh,
smile, laugh and applaud.

"The Rich Man gave them a bag of gold
and everyone cheered on the day
the church had a new bell."
The couple are starched in best white –
as the singing swells, they marry
and claim their gold.
It is intensely sad and fleetingly
realises the ghosts of our innocence.

Flashlights – the year's frozen
for this instant.
Keep that – don't move – stay there,
stay somewhere like that for ever.

It all builds to The Nativity:
Joseph, Mary and the three glittering Kings
change without age, time after time.
Only the baby Jesus doll remains,

a scarred and worn wooden face held magically
fresh each year in the laundered swaddling.
The audience – parents and children in arms,
grandparents and neighbours, point and giggle,
there's a glow and, finally, we all sing.

This has worked some sort of renewal,
some sort of an ending.

Five Andrew Wyeth Poems

1. Andrew Wyeth at The Royal Academy

How close can we get?
A German tourist in front of me
leans over the rope to Wyeth's
Witching Hour
The world swings from its hook.

He stretches as if to touch the canvas.
His fingers dance around
the six chairs then rise
to the blown candelabra's
guttering smoke and flames.
They instantly clench like burnt moths.

His hand returns to his side,
spreads and wipes itself down his trouser leg

2. Spring Fed

the stone basin
fills and fills
from the swivel tap's
trickle.

The hills have shed
so much snow
and now,
the first brown grasses
clear of it,
the heifers push
up into the fields
to take the early shoots.

And it comes
again
the whole slow
turning of the season –
the softer touch of air,
the shine on the bucket,
the unclenching of things,
the lapping of the water
in the stone basin
up to the rim,
and the very first,
this
delicious overspilling
onto our boots.

3. Pine Baron

The spiky swift gestures
of an avenue of pines
and under them, this still-life:

the helmet Karl Kuerner wore on the Marne,
a sniper decorated by the Crown Prince.
Here his wife Anna uses it as a scuttle

loaded with dry cones to start her fires.
It is part of their farm now,
like a bucket or a cooking pot.

But what brings my jeep
jamming to a halt
right by that helmet on its brown blanket of needles

are the pitchy ridges of the cones,
with the sheen of oiled feathers, the curve of ears.
– They burn like a dream – she says.

4. Chambered Nautilus

Becalmed in her bed,
her face turned shining towards
the twelve panes of her window,
hands clenched around her knees,
she rides the big four-poster under the full canopy,
a sailing ship lulled
in crossing the twelve oceans.

She has a basket of papers, and light.
She has the pearl conch, a full, fluted ear
where the salt water breaks over and over,
the tides pull and run
anytime she needs them to.

And she does not have to wait long
for it is happening, the stir of water,
the wind's pulse.
And it is ready
her ship, her bed, her ark.

5. Winter 1946

The hill is in breath
like the flank of an animal.
Beyond, the fields of wintery grass,
a spiked hedge that roots
to the actual.

Along the fence-line
grooves of late snow
are crossed with slant shadows.
The air is brittle,
rare and thin in your lungs.

You appear as a wartime flier
in buttoned corduroy coat
walking away from his crash;
under the flaps of your winter helmet
your face pale as egg-shell.

Weight forward and to your right,
you are about to run down the hill
into the known future.
Your shadow trails like smoke,
your hand flapping in the air.

•

And my feeling of being disconnected from everything.
Over the other side of that hill
was where my father was killed
and I was sick I'd never painted him.
The hill became a portrait of him.

Letter to John Digby on Long Island

The Gatsby mansions sit snug in this snow.
Sea Cliff bay has frozen –
ice wedged over what is,
for all I know, a beach,
the memory of waves.

You're a recluse, you say,
and here that's nothing new.
Your work – cutting and measuring,
breaking up pictures
to fit the one in your head.

"I hate this bloody America, you know."
All Winter cooped up on Maple Avenue,
your scalpel sliced open Victorian skies,
birds inside landscapes inside birds,
pinned butterflies of the surreal.

Now football turns to cricket without your knowing.
I wish you a year of red cardinals, nut-thatch –
let your paper eagles rise to the trees.
You've written Joan's valentine in the porch snow,
John, go – make your own lovely, crazy way into Spring!

Lines for Hanlyn Davies

(written between Brattleboro and Bellow Falls. January 1980)

Sixteen years over here and still you watch
for Swansea's score in *The New York Times*.
What do we leave behind us when we leave –
are we passing up a nation for hamburgers and crime?

Back home they're burning houses in the country,
the hoses on the language see it drown.
The Devolution Vote is just a sour memory,
we're singing for another Triple Crown.

The language and the rugby are romance,
a ragged tapestry we patch and stitch.
Taking the plane is a paradigm –
throwing the marriage but loving the bitch.

The farther away, the less we're sure.
Your prints, these words, are codes of discontent.
We'll change the world by adding to it:
to know where you're from, and why you went.

That Last Evening

you stayed on late into the night –
repairs in the workshop,
fixing the parts,
what you'd always done best.

Sat hunched over the bench
with the crescent ache of the lung wound
bending you into yourself,
you count the tools back into the rack.

In the morning you'd be gone,
the flesh globing to your skull,
lips strung tight from the swollen gums.
A streak of shit on your pyjamas.

Driving home that night,
the last time you would see the ocean
and still no closer to knowing
what engineered the waves,

why those curls of surf
rise and topple on the beach.
Imagine being unhorsed by
the clumsy arc of a peasant's scythe.

My Grandmother's Cactus

This cactus is shooting points out
from the desk at the centre of my room.
I bought it for you in the Fifties,
a kid's odd present from the Royal Welsh Show.

Gran, you grew as prickly as the plant,
had feuds with neighbours and family,
were confused by quarrels and gossip.
Now that dumb plant's outlasted you.

This year it thrives under the sun-facing window.
All that time on your window-sill held it back,
stunted by the lack of sun
through your half-drawn curtains.

In twenty years it flowered twice –
pink, delicate flowers like anemones
nestling in the clumps of needles.
And sometimes the arms would canker and darken.

With the bad cut away it grew out
wide and angled crazily from the trunk.
Time after time, when I'm sunk in work
and stretch for a book, I'm spiked.

The needles stab through shirts and
wool and cloth. The jabs hook under the skin
and days later inflame as spots that weep poison.
I should move it. I should throw it out.

But Gran, it's part of you in my life.
One day I will, in turning to the shelf,
thinking of quite different things,
put my face right into it – that sure pain.

The Freezer

When they finally broke in
the place smelled like Pompeii –
dust, ash, fall-out inches thick.
She was sitting there, a queen propped
up in bed and not looking so hot.

In the garage an A.C.
road racer from the '30s worth thousands –
quality coachwork under the dust, and not a scratch.

All types of fungi in the kitchen
but the freezer was stocked and neat –
twenty-nine stiff cats packed and labelled:
"Roland" – "Katherine" – "Veronique" –
and so on, reading like a list of social
acquaintances. Curled, stretched, flat or sprung,
as if the shape gave each one a character.

The next evening, mackerel-eyed, fur
stuck like old pasting brushes,
they got shovelled into the garden.

The green eye of the freezer glowed,
the frosted chest purred and shuddered
in the empty house
until they cut off the mains.

Veteran: South Dakota 1978

If you were in demolition
taking out the bridges
as the marines fell back.
If you were ordered to cut down
the women and kids,
leave everything dead.
If you swung round like
the workings of a clock
and scythed the three officers instead,
fragged them good –
if all that's true,
then I'm with you.

But if saying this is your trick,
your way of living
with the fact you'd really
killed those peasants
(given the war and the VC
and not knowing
one gook from another
and it's making a better story that way)
then this party is flaking off
from your head like used skin
and I'm far from home
and reason and the neat confusions
that make poetry.

Trials

I believe nothing of this.
Nothing.

Lies infest these proceedings like lice
– a court of blind revenge.
You talk to me of gas chambers
– show me them.
Photographs – faked.
A man in Dusseldorf wrote me –
Ah! You don't listen.

Hermione – she is my wife.
A loving wife since the time she came
to the United States of America.
She is a citizen these long years.
Like me – an American.
How should I believe these lies?
Revenge and emotion runs wild in there
– even in the public gallery a Jew
dressed in the striped-pyjama camp things.

She worked in the office I tell you
– files, typing, numbers and lists.

So how could there be justice?

Ach – they say eight hundred and twenty
thousand pairs of shoes.
Jewelry, teeth, gold teeth,
a mountain of wedding rings. Where?
Show me these things – the proof.

Who kills children must be animals.
You believe that –
kicking them to death;
the Harvest Festival of open graves;
a German Shepherd off the leash tearing
a pregnant woman apart –
all the stuff of propaganda,
horror stories of the Zionists.

Enough of this Maidanek. Let it rest.

American Jews want these trials.
That Wiesenthal is a crazy man.
A hunter for thirty years – he
should learn to forget.
Let them all go to Phnom Penh, Uganda, the Russians,
– let them put their scruples to the test.
All I know is that for me
it will be years more without her.
Can you understand the horror of that?

One night a blanket of snow
thick over the State of New York; the lines
down. I go with her in my dreams:
she moves ahead of me, turning
in the saddle, beckoning now
with her whip. She moves towards
the smoke rising in the trees, past
a straggling column of refugees.

Hermione, my wife, my woman,
my beautiful silver mare.

First-class in the Hold

This is a calm Channel crossing
into the dark, early morning. Two a.m.
I'm purblind, lenses out, shoes off,
dazed and falling asleep on the tilting floor.
So are hundreds more on three decks,
like some community pageant of Dante.
The corpses stir as we plough towards Cherbourg,
this last half-hour roughening up,
the ship rolling like an old lover
churning in her own space and time.

To clear my head, to shape
up for the long night's drive south,
I need a book and pull out *Life Studies* –
the Lowells of Beverly Farms and Dunbarton graveyard.
Seven decades and four thousand miles away
that Boston family's declining days
compose a poet's litany of his beginnings.
And then 'Sailing Home from Rapallo'
when the shoreline broke
into fiery flower and Lowell's
Mother travelled first-class,
her funeral casket in the hold.

Elbows at the rail,
I blink and lean out into the dark.
The air slaps like a cold towel,
lights gleam from the foreign coast.
Below, someone calls out in French.

In the car-hold, under the sour-cream lamps,
we belt ourselves safely in.
Robert Lowell, now I remember how you died –
a Manhattan yellow cab, your heart gave out.

I never met or even saw you read
but it's clear your ghost rides
in the poets that survive:
Heaney, Walcott, Dunn,
write your continuing elegy.
Unsettled spirit, I'd gladly have
you shoulder me.

I start the engine as the bow yawns open.
The only lights at the end of that tunnel
are the docks and then back streets,
muted and dull.

We crawl down the map into Brittany:
place-names realised in empty squares
the Michelin doesn't gloss.
Unlit bistros and bars
all the way down until Ploërmel
where we find hot, strong coffee
and the morning's first croissants –
ordering like tourists, self-consciously,
stumbling and tasting the words.

So much of what we aim at is style:
all the while the lever presses down espresso grains
and the patron's Gaulloise jigs on his lips,
I'm holding onto half-remembered lines –
Beverly Farms to West Street to Marlborough, and then,
Marlborough Street, West Street, Rapallo
and Dunbarton graveyard again.

Jack Watts

squints across a sprouting field,
chews at a leaf, then weighs your crop
to the nearest bag.

Soft cap down to the eyes
and what had been somebody's suit
held by baling cord;
he is pigmented with dirt
as if washing would have drained
away the years' knowledge.

The whole county waits:
in April the Pembrokeshire Earlies come
a stiff, dark green out of the ground.
Jack and his tribe pour
like Winter rats from their cottage.

Jack stops at the stile,
pushes the cap back to the perch of his head,
then walks along a row to what becomes
the centre of the field.
He delivers a potato from the earth,
soil spilling from the web of tubers,
shaking from the clumps.
He scrapes through dirt and skin;
the sweet flesh goes between his leather lips,
a nugget lodging in the jags of his teeth.

He closes his eyes on the taste –
it is the soil crumbling, the crush
of frost, the rain carried in on the sea,
the sweat of planting.

He holds the ridged sweetness to his nose,
between finger and thumb it glistens,
the rarest egg, the first
potato and the last.

Pembrokeshire Seams

Wales is a process.
Wales is an artefact which the Welsh produce.
The Welsh make and remake Wales
day by day, year by year, generation after generation
if they want to.
                    – Gwyn A.Williams

1.

Between Wiseman's Bridge and Saundersfoot
the coast path runs into coal wagon tunnels
and entrance holes drift down
into the base of a sheer cliff.
A pair of rails points from the path's edge
to launch the memory of themselves out over the bay
in perfect alignment with the next tunnel.

The children run on round: in the dark
there are hollows the shape of a body
they press themselves into. They
burst out at us like predictable ghosts
and we chase them into the light.

On the sand strip below us
the storm has flung a crop
of rotting star-fish.

2.

Those years I lived down here,
my parents let the bungalow to English visitors
and we spent the Summers in two damp caravans.

We dug the garden patch for potatoes
and the hedge-bank would crumble
with dark shale, flaky stuff on its way
down the centuries to coal.
On a high fire you could coax it
to smoulder and flame.

3.

Coal was under us all the time,
the tail of the South Wales seam
surfacing again after the sea.
Shallow, tricky minings worked by families;
the men and children bunched like rats at the levels,
the women at a windlass winching up each
basket of good anthracite with a bent back.
Faults cracked and connived at the work –

this land never saw the rape of the valleys,
though the farmers' sons, worn by the rain
and sick of the smell of the shippen,
walked east and fed the deep pits and the iron.
On day trips their children's children
made their way back, built castles on the beach.

4.

My people – the Barrahs, the Thomases
raised cattle and potatoes
on good farming land from Llangwm to Jeffreyston.
Until my great-grandfather
that night in 1908
drunk and late from Narberth market,
roaring down the dark lanes, snapped his pony's leg
and turned the trap over his neck.
Six daughters, and a renegade son away in Canada,
saw the farm sold and split.

We lose ourselves down the years.

Under the earth at Jeffreyston,
wood groans, crack of the bones' cocoon.
A name smoothed away from the slant headstone.

5.

To the north, in the next county,
cottages are put to the torch for the language,
for the idea of community.

A Range Rover coasts to the end of the lane;
shadows, murmurs, a burning bottle
clatters through mock-Georgian panes.
Rebecca rises to purify the tribe.

Not here; below the Landsker
we've been eased out of such extremes.

6.

It is a Summer's day. The sea burns
against the eye.
A sky full of laughter and fat gulls.

On the boat to Caldey Island,
looking back you see the fields glint.
The windscreens on the cliff
pearl like standing water.
Deep down lanes a crop of caravans;
sites flower like clumps of nettles.

We trail our hands in the sea.
What did we imagine they would hold?
In the shock of cold they whiten
to the beauty of bones, of coral.

Land Army Photographs

How lumpy and warlike you all looked,
leaning against the back of a truck,
hair permed underneath head scarves;
in make-up, corduroys, with long woollen socks
– the uniform completed by a khaki shirt and tie.

You are posed in a harvest field:
long wooden rakes and open necks in one
of those hot wartime summers. Fifteen of you
squinting into the camera,
and the weaselly Welsh farmer, arms folded,
his cap set at an angle
that would be jaunty for anyone else.
He's sitting there in the middle, not really
knowing about Hitler, or wanting to know,
but glad to have all those girls
with their English accents and their laughs.

Mother, how young you look, hair back, dungarees,
a man's head at your shoulder.
You girls cleared scrub-land, burned gorse,
eyes weeping as the smoke blew back;
milked cows and watched pigs slaughtered.
You, who could not drive,
drove tractors with spiked metal wheels, trucks.
And once, on the Tenby to Pembroke road,
along the Ridgeway, they had you working flax.
For two days only it bloomed,
the most delicate blue flowers.
Like wading into a field of water.

I see you piling the gorse. Dried spikes
flaring into silver ferns, and smoke

twisting from the piles as the wind comes in
gusts, cool from the sea, the gulls drifting
lazily on the flow.

                    And then,
one of them, too steady, too level, becoming
a Sunderland coasting in to Milford Haven:
over Skomer, Skokholm, Rat Island, over the deep water;
and, though you do not know it, over a man
who is smoking, scraping field potatoes
for the searchlight crew's supper,
who pulls and unpeels the rabbit they have trapped,
joints and throws it into the steaming stew,
the oil-drum perched over an open fire;
the man who looks up, the man who is my father,
watching the white belly of that flying boat
cut into the Haven.

The World

This is how it ends:

a finger slips –
two Russian subs resurrected
from the ocean
retaliate
before they drown.

California
the flat Mid-West
the Great Lakes cities
New York/Washington
– all clouds, acid air.
Europe's on fire.
The Third World eats
itself and starves.

In the far North
the Inuit
listen to their radios.
They move further North and
the North wind sweeps them clean.

This is how it ends

with the last family of Inuit
eating fallen caribou
pushing North
killing sick bears
going West.
Reaching the Bering Straits:
at the edge of the ice

a bloated seal at their feet.
And farther out floating
towards them on a floe
a man, a woman and child waving
spears.

Tortoise

They bought you a tortoise and every Autumn your father packed it away in its Winter box of straw in the house-loft. One year, in the late Spring, you climbed up to find the box empty. You all searched the grimy space, finding nothing and coming down dirty as sweeps.

Years later, your mother writes that four houses further along the terrace they've found a shell in the loft. Just that. A shell, hard, perfect and whole. Inside, a shrunk ball of jelly.

The image makes you shiver for days, then it lodges in the back of your mind. To travel and come to nothing, leaving behind something shaped, hard and scoured out: an object which no longer holds you or needs you, being finished, and what it was always growing towards.

Worm

The slow-worm I found
in the vortex of cuttings
is cool and still in my hand –
a sliver of mercury
a coiled spring
a silver choker laid
above the curve of a breast
that wants to be touched
and rises with breath.

Cold blood in a wire
sinuous and alive
it turns a thick whip
bulks like a hawser
at that moment
it's released from the ship
weighing its length heavily
casually through air
before creasing a white edge
through the oily water.

Could this be one of the lords of life?
I don't know.
I value though the cool line
printed across my palm
and place this poor snake gently
in a tangle of ivy and privet
near the crumbling wall
out of harm.
For there are cats
and crows to claw the scales
from its length and we need
such things by
us in the final house
– attending spirits
an amulet
a charm.

Two For Luck

The morning started badly –
A thin frost, damp on the plugs,

One magpie rising off the railway crossing
As the gates rattled shut for the Sunday milk crawler.

The car-park jammed full at the club.
Driven pegs snapping on the first tee.

Then on the seventh fairway,
At the top of his backswing,

The knife pushed out of his chest
And somehow he knew what to do –

Lowered his six iron and walked in
To the clubhouse with an "Excuse me."

Drove steadily home and said quite firmly:
"Phone for Henderson at the surgery,

And an ambulance, I'm going to have
An attack."

"But ... why ...?"
"Give me air," he said,

And walked out on the patio
Measuring his pace, avoiding the cracks.

Opaquely through a lifting haze, the sun glowed
On the new leaves, the tight crowns of apple-blossom.

He stooped to pull a weed
And caught the smell of earth.

He stood there until they arrived to lay
Him between the red blankets, knees drawing

Up to the foetal position, one hand
In his wife's hand, the other

Fisting at his chest and
The blades working like beaks

Against the breast-cage, all the way
As they sirened across town

To the bed where the mask closed over him.
They said – "Sleep."

And he dreamed of that approach like a bullet,
The ball biting and holding up to the lip of the cup,

His long walk across the green
To life aloft the pin flying the black

And white body of a dead magpie
Its wingfeathers edged wih the sharpest blue.

Field of Wheat

Out from the storming night they came
and before them the field bowed
over to the sky and fell towards the sea.
Rich and gold, the wheat settled like hair
though the facing slope was shadowed at its centre.

See, how the wheat is broken and flattened there
she said – that must have been the storm.
But then, why just at that point?

He said – that's a fox after a hare,
some hunted creature flushed from cover.

No! I want an older spirit,
Branwen, daughter of Llyr, escaped from Ireland
and running across a Welsh field.

He turned back into the room – some freak
of wind, some current eddying down.
This room's a mess. Let's tidy up.

No wind's scythe, but two lovers thrashing
in the field – she said
as we have done.

He shook down the quilt with peacocks
– Stay close to me in my life, you
and your imagination.

The Last Candles

The final stage of our journey over
we reached Odessa. So glorious
a scene I think my eyes had never taken in –
the harbour bristling with ships of all the allied nations.
We were received at the consulate by a young man,
fresh and clean in a crisp English suit.
Courteous and gentlemanly. I had not seen
such a man for three years.

In the hotel that night my dreams were of uniforms
and wounds, but one wound served for many –
thus, a severed arm at Biyech, the lacerated
stomach of a boy in Khutanova, the bloody head
of a captured Turk in Noscov – and then swabs
fell like the first snows of Winter,
the land chill and beyond pain
under its bandages.

For breakfast we were offered white bread and an egg!
The smell of coffee made me dizzy.

At nine we leave for the harbour. The streets
packed with aimless crowds, though everything
makes way for the *Bolsheviki* in their lorries.
At the harbour gates a man of no apparent rank
holds our papers for an hour.
He has a rifle and a long knife hangs
from his belt. A red band has been clumsily
sewn to the sleeve of his coat.

Some of the Norwegian crew speak English.
My cabin proves small, but warm.
After years under canvas, sheltering in ruins,
nursing beneath shattered roofs,
I am glad to call it home.
Though the place is strange and metallic
after stone and wood and earth.

Doctor Rakhil calls to take me on deck
for our departure.
                        Ten years of living in this great land
have brought me to love it.
Though three of those years have been spent in war,
and then this anarchy, this revolution.
I see Odessa under red flags
as we cast off and the engines churn.
I feel everything moving away from me
as if Russia were a carpet being rolled to the sky.
At the harbour mouth Doctor Rakhil
gently turns me from the rail,
but is not quite quick enough.

That night, the sea pressing around me,
I dream of three things –
                        a day
in Moscow, when Nadya and I
were close enough to reach out and touch
the Tsar, and an old peasant
who had crawled through the crowd, between
the legs of the guards, clutching
his ragged petition,

still calling out as their boots struck him.
Nicholas II, Tsar of all the Russias, flickered
his eyes, but his step was the unfaltering
step of a god.
                    My first dead man
in the training ward. Grey and small in the candlelight,
his mouth like a closed purse and what seemed
to be butterflies on his face. Two sugarlumps
to weigh down his eye-lids.
                            And at last, this leaving
Odessa. How in the shadows I saw them –
officers from the front fleeing the chaos of desertion
and caught by the Reds at the port.
They bound their feet to heavy stones
and planted them in the harbour. Swaying, grey shapes
I glimpsed from the rail, as if
bowing to me.
The last candles of my Russia
guttering and going out under the black sea.

Narrative from *A Nurse on the Russian Front 1914-18* by Florence Farnborough.

Games with my Daughter

The first clear afternoon of Spring bursts
April's buds and bulbs in the park.
This year when I catch and take her weight
she powers the swing and arcs
from finger-stretch behind my head
to soaring feet-in-the-clouds.
Mothers to our left and right
shrink in their corridors of safe flight.

Our game's revealed the filling out,
the firmer, young woman's stare,
the promise Winter concealed beneath its coat.
Forward and up she splits the sky, each
swing down and back she goes by to where
my tip-toed fingers' grasp can't reach.

Villanelle for a Photographer

O. Winston Link: *Hot Shot East at Iaeger,*
West Virginia, August 1956

The smooching couple in the chrome saloon
Are teasing love in their fumbling way
As the Norfolk & Western steams before an August moon.

On the drive-in screen a wounded MIG plumes
Through a cold-war sky. Strategic blunders will betray
The smooching couple in the chrome saloon

Whose earnest gropings, sighs and moans
Counterpoint the loco's thrust and sway
As the Norfolk & Western steams before an August moon.

Link's wired-up lamps, set to jewel the gloom,
Flashlight the upholstered Fifties and display
The smooching couple in the chrome saloon.

What gung-ho promise drowns in a Korean monsoon
While marines act out some crude screenplay?
As the Norfolk & Western steams before an August moon,

Like train-crossed lovers in a soft-top tomb,
These clean-cut kids compose their dream, in a Chevrolet,
The smooching couple in the chrome saloon
As the Norfolk & Western steams before an August moon.

Thoughts from the Holiday Inn

for John Tripp

"When you're dead, you're bloody dead."
We both liked the punch of that one, John, said
Ten or more years ago by an author breaking
Through his fiction, kicking the rules, risking
All our willing disbelief to shock through
To the truth. B.S. Johnson, that sad and tortured man, knew
The whole thing to be by turns a joke, by turns the need
To love each other into something close to sense. We bleed,
John, we bleed, and time bleeds from our wrists.
Your death was shocking, and tidies up another lovely, angry
      (when pissed),
Poet of a man, who would not, for anyone, be tidied into
      respectability
Longer than an evening, or his allotment in some anthology.
There's too much to be said, by too many, too soon.
But from this lunchtime watering place, this unlikeliest of rooms,
Spare me the modest time and space – by Christ, you've enough
Of both in death, old mate – to work things out, sound off –
About the months you've missed, the months that we've missed you.
You'd have seen this place go up, the skyline that you knew
Transformed, jagged, blocked as urban planners brought rationality
To what the coal century had grown and shaped to the Taff's
      estuary.
We've needed you here, John, thrusting out your neck and
      stroking the chin
From a classy, fraying shirt to show the disdain we hold these
      people in,
These late-comers to a country and a nation in a mess.
They've given us the bum's rush today, John, I must confess.
We checked out the place for next year's Literature Festival
And sponsorship. As far as we could tell
It was a waste of time, for any management

Who'd given Sickle-Cell Research the thumbs down were clearly
    bent
On profit, and to hell with charity, never mind cultural P.R.
Well fed and disappointed, we returned to the bar.
Still, they'd named the two big function rooms, the 'Dylan Suite'
And 'Gwyn Jones Room'. "Don't know him," said the manageress,
    with complete
Honesty. "He's one of our Academy's most distinguished senior
    members,"
I said, and thought, We do no more than blow upon the embers,
We scribblers who'd want to claim
That everything in Wales for praise or blame
Is brought to life and fact and mythical creation
By that writerly mix of ego and the grasp of a tradition.
What use we prove, the weight the world gives us, if any,
Is likely to be cheap and grudging, no more than a blunt penny
Flung to shut our mannered, metred whining.
Then, later, taken up again shining
From the rubbing our tongues and lives impart.
I hear you answer, John, "It's a start, boy, some sort of bloody start."
John, further down the Hayes, now I think of you, haunting those
    benches
And passing a coffee or the length of a fag below the rich stenches
From Brains's brewery snugged in behind the Royal Arcade.
As the big internationals move in and build and build the shade
And sunlight shift position down the city's roads.
In spruced-up Bute (re-named, as Tiger Bay encodes
A docklands past we'd best forget or sanitise)
In tarted-up pubs or tree-lined low-rise
Flats – *The Jolly Tar* or *Laskar's Close*.
The men who clinch the deals, the gaffers, the boss
With the tax-free Daimler, the Series Seven,
Square out the mazy city into real estate concepts, proven

Returns for their money. They are gilt-edged applicants
For Euro-funds, Welsh Development grants.
This hotel is for the likes of them. It stretches eye to eye
With the brewery's silver funnel, two hundred bedrooms in the sky
Starting at fifty quid the night. "Fat cats," I hear you say,
"And that's before your breakfast. Stuff the fucking pool, O.K."
Tax payer's rage? John, even you, an occasional connoisseur
Of hotel fitments and glimpses of the soft life, would incur
A gullet-sticking at this pricey junk, mock-Grecian style
Arches, columns, thick marble-facings done in tiles,
Plush, deep divans around an open fire beneath a metal canopy,
Surrogate logs you'd hardly warm your hands upon. You'd see
Beyond, the indoor pool, functional, gaunt,
More marble, sharp angles with, each end, broken columns to flaunt
The facile version of classic decor money'll buy
And set down in a city anywhere, across a sky
Or ocean. Continent to continent there must be travellers
Who need the reassurance of such nondescript pools and bars.
To step off the plane or train, taxi down concrete tracks
To what the Telex reservation guarantees predictable: stacks
Of credit-cards accepted, pool-side temperature just O.K.
An in-house movie they choose and relay
To each room in American or English – God forbid
The native patois – (*These people down here, the Welsh – did*
You say – a language all their own – an ancient tongue?
– King Arthur – well, I saw a movie when I was a kid, sang
The songs all that summer – Dannie Kaye – got it!)
John, what kind of progress is all this shit?
They took the coal-miners and put 'em in a coal museum:
And the people drove down, coughed up three quid ten just to
      see 'em.
Tourists one-nighting en route the Beacons, Bath or Ireland:

"Cardiff – what's that?" "The airport.. . it's halfways there. I planned
To break the trudge from Heathrow." And what of the locals?
Lunchtimes bring yuppies of both sexes, the gals
Waft in like *Cosmo* covers, the men have knife-
Creased casuals, hook their index fingers through the keyrings of life.
And there's the mid-day nibblers, women past their prime
But dressed to the nines and painted, passing the time
Between Howells' upholstery and Hones and Jones with a small gin
And sandwich triangles of horseradish and smoked salmon,
Piquant, hardly fattening. Their cigarette smoke curls
Away with the suggestion of rope, these former good-lookers, girls
Who, thirty years before, bagged a man of promise or means
And moved up, to Cyncoed, out to Lisvane, a pool, lawns
Done by a man who brings his own machine and strips
His shirt in the long afternoons. They tip
Him with the last cut of September.
Their husbands are on the board and successfully bored.
        "Remember,"
They'd say, "when we had that little semi in Newport,
And we'd spend Sundays, you mowing and me trimming." "I've fought
Hard to get this far, and Christ, there's times I wonder,
What for? What have we got? Where's it gone? Just blunder
On to the next rung, dinner party, contract, barbeque."
"Love, you're working too hard. Is the company proving too
        much for you?"
John, excuse this indulgence, that clumsy fiction, it's no digression,
I'm still concerned to understand progression.
When working-class is all you've known
These rich fish cruise by bright-coloured (if overblown)
Distracting – but these too are tenants of the pool

You plunged your wit and pen into. Fool
No-one was your aim, and at last came the anger of *Life Under
        Thatcher.*
But winos in the Hayes betray a watcher
Who'd sum up the whole state of things in verses.
It's too easy to shoot off steam in curses
That pepper the mark but fail to penetrate.
Guys with real assets, clever portfolios, are immune to street hate;
They justify themselves in terms of respectability, vision,
        advancement.
The world's an oyster if you lift your nose off the pavement.
They've bought themselves out of the firing line.
Windows purr close, revs slipping the motor into fifth gear, it feels
        fine
To loosen out along the motorway – weekends in Pembs
Or, turning right, over the Bridge, a trim two hours to dine by the
        Thames.
No-one's rooted anymore, John, as you must have known –
"The old man" coming to smith in Taffs Well in the '30s where
        you'd grown
Up Welsh, not Cornish like him, in all but the language.
(The wounding of that loss, it seems, no achievements can assuage.)
And, because of that, confused, determined and concerned
As the rest of us, excluded from the Gorsedd but feeling you'd
        earned
The right to sound off for this Wales – Taffs and Gwerin,
To voice the peculiar place of the eighty per cent. The din
Of justified protest settled after '79 – Welsh cheque books,
        Channel Four.
The nationalist drummings the Sixties saw you working for
You realised later were too easy, too raw. Like R.S.
You loved the country with a passion, an anger, but the less

Misty, period-costume work will surely prove the best,
The more enduring; real poetry "welcoming the rough-weather
     guest".
John, I would rather have seen your ashes ebb from Barafundle
Bay. That grey day at Thornhill we watched your coffin trundle
Behind the curtains to the kind of anonymity
You'd rail against for other "botched angels", losers we
Turn away from, society's mistakes, the hard-done-to,
Underdogs you wanted to feel close to.
The glow of a cupped-hand fag was light enough to draw
You to some alley, a derelict huddled there against a door,
One of the Hollow Men, a voter with no vote
Wrapped in old woollens, Echoes stuffed inside an overcoat.
"Cold enough, butt, eh? on the street. Here, have yourself a cuppa.
Take care, old fella, and watch out for the copper.
Those bastards aren't for the likes of us,
They don't give a tinker's cuss
As long as things stay down and quiet, and everything's neat.
You and me'll keep to the shadows, butt, and stay light on our
     feet."
I've a feeling poetry's not the thing most apt
To dissect society, or politicise an audience one imagines trapped
In wilful ignorance, lobotomised by the trashy press,
Disenfranchised by the soapy box, seduced by the caress
Of the goodish life in the second half of this softening century.
You, fellow sprinter, took your chance through readings – could be
Five or fifty listeners, in club, gallery, college, school.
But articles in the London nationals, plays on the t.v. as a rule
Work most action, albeit short-lived. We
Poets light shower-burning fuses or rockets you see
Flash and quickly fade as the moment's charged
And spent. John, you saw the first decade of this city enlarged,

Pulled into the dream-shape someone thought we needed.
At fifty-nine who's to say you'd not changed things, not succeeded
In stirring up whatever stuff this corner of the pool had in
        suspension?
Talk of booze, too little care taken of yourself, prevention
Of the heart's explosion that took you in the early hours
With McGuigan's fight won and the tele drizzling showers
Of grey flakes down its mute screen,
Won't bring you back. You slid away. The barely-tuned machine
Packed up. Unlike Dylan, no insult to the brain, John. Often we'd talk
Of going to the States, whistle-stopping, the Chelsea in New York,
Our tour for the Yanks, I could have rigged.
Yes, if I'd pushed it, we two in tandem could have gigged
Over there. Like a lot of the others, I chickened out, I suppose.
Pembrokeshire a couple of nights – you with no change of clothes,
Just a battered attache, poems, toothbrush, fags –
Was the limit of my stamina for your ways. Memory drags
Such petty guilts to the fore.
Though I treasure and feed off that reading we did on the man o' war,
Reluctant sailors pouring export ale down us
To forestall the poetry (they did) drown us
With hospitality in the middle of Fishguard harbour
Until we staggered past the missiles in her belly's store
Up to the frigate's redundant forward gun-turret, officers dressed
In cummerbunds, and elegant women. The talk was veiled, but
        impressed
Words like 'Responsibility', 'Capability' and 'Global role'. "Yes, but
What do you do with all this training? All the missiles, shit-hot
Fire-power?" I remember, he answered you with, "We can blow
        Fishguard
Away with each one, you know. We are, I suppose, a 'hard
Fist gloved by our democratic masters'." John, before the evening
        ended

You topped that with a poem scribbled on a cigarette pack. We descended
    descended
A precarious ladder to the launch with those lines of his and yours
    sinking
Into the night. And now, a decade later, the story has a ring
Any writer could tune. Perhaps that's what your Sandeman Port
    inquisitor
Pointed to – after the jaunts and applause, the writer's for
Filling the void, putting structure into space, a kind of race
Against apathy and oblivion. Too grand, you say, too heroic? Let's
    face
It, John, we've both indulged in our 'intervals of heat'
On the page and off. Both been chilled by the thought one couldn't
    beat
The odds – stuck in Wales, chiselling verse, weak in the flesh.
We're out on the edge of the world's concern, no Wall St, no
    Long Kesh.
Unless the challenge here is also to connect – radar dishes at
    Brawdy,
Hinkley over the water, Trawsfynydd, the poison brought in on our
    sea.
An *Anglo*, dipped in England's sewer should still produce the goods.
Albeit in "invisible ink / on dissolving paper . . ." one loads
The futile quarto, pushes it out to travel or sink.
Standing here before the Holiday Inn, and its shiny 0-3-0, I think
How my grandfather, before the Great War, shunted down to Wales
    on the G.W.R.
How arbitrary one's identity is: with voice and gesture we are
Challenged to make sense of where and what we find ourselves. No
Border guards patrol the Dyke, no frontier seals us in at Chepstow.
Did you really ever want that, John, seriously?
From here I have to question that stance. Were you quite as you
    appeared to be?

This locomotive worked the sidings in Cardiff and the junction,
Was scrapped at Barry and now is made to function
As an image of our hard-bitten history. *9629*, freshly painted green
    and black,
Her valves de-gutted, holds to her half-dozen yards of track:
No driver on the footplate, no steam, no destination,
This featureless hotel her final station,
Under the flags of Canada, Commerce and the Dragon.
I turn around. On the island in the Hayes a wino tilts his flagon
And light flashes from the moment.

Wind from the Sea

a villanelle for Andrew Wyeth

Wind from the sea
Takes the stale net curtain in its teeth
And the shreds stream away from me.

The woven birds caught in its vagary
Are lifted and shaken by the force beneath
Wind from the sea.

The frayed curtain composes a plea –
Men o' War blossom like sailors' wreaths
And the shreds stream away from me;

The torn lace prints a skeleton tree
Against grey skies that drown belief.
Wind from the sea

Lances over the forest of pines, see –
It drives and cuts without relief
And the shreds stream away from me.

Stand at the window, stare to infinity,
What's promised will prove the leavings of a thief –
Wind from the sea –
And the shreds stream away from me.

Summer in Greece

Each day at noon the Englishman
drives into the sea.
He uses a seven-iron and places the balls
on a strip of carpet which he carries rolled
under his arm from the villa. A dozen
or two small splashes in the ocean.
They sink and cluster in the sand
gleaming like the hearts of opened sea-urchins.

Later, when it is cool, the boys swim out
and dive. They gather the balls –
Dunlop, Slazenger, Titleist, Penfold –
and return to the village. These are eggs
you can't crack or eat. They bounce.
There are no golf courses here.

Some mornings the Englishman from the villa
buys golf balls from the village.
They are cheap and the supply is constant.

The Emerald

I stayed at the palace for the last three days
where he lay on a great bed
with its four pillars of solid silver shaped
as four naked women holding *punkahs*.

At the end they lifted him down and laid him
on a simple mat of straw and grasses –
from the level earth a man rises to greatness
and at the last the greatest of such will return

to a common ground.
As his final breath escaped there
came a noise such as I had never heard
nor wish again to hear.

The women's cries, rising to a wail,
an eerie keening that cut
through the endless passages of that place.
This is the very sound of death, I thought.

In leaving I passed their room
and finding the door ajar, I entered
for the first and only time
that private place – zenana.

The Maharanees were entranced and swayed
in the wake of their wailing.
I took a step inside and felt myself losing
my feet – the floor was treacherously aflame!

Encrusted like a carpet in a fable –
for it is the Hindu way that women let fall
their jewels to the ground in loss.
A king's ransom lay there, stopped short of his soul.

Filling the pockets of my suit
would have bought me a title back
here in England. I stooped
once. A large emerald.

My last wish is – keep this
as the memory of my years in India.
This alone is for you and your daughters
after you from my time in the service.

Wear it clear and public on your
breasts. A stolen thing, a remembrance.
We British, we are
a people beyond the humility of straw.

From the City That Shone

The thing we dreamt of most was a bath:
so we crossed the wire and made for Gonnelieu
where, it was said, a tin bath lay abandoned
near the well of the convent school.
We kept to ruined shadows down the street,
towels and soap in our haversacks.

John had a canvas bucket and filled it from the well.
The bath held firm, the water cold and sweet.
I lorded it there in the weedy garden
amidst the ransacked books strewn all about,
broken glass wicked in the sun,
then towelled dry while
John tipped the water across the grass.

I drew fresh water for him and passed the soap.
"I always sing," he said.
"Too risky," I said.
But he splashed and hummed
– *And who shall kiss her ruby lips*
When I am far away? –

I sat on the path, my hair drying,
my head thrown back to the clearing sky
where a Taube stuttered through clouds from the West.
In those moments before the guns started up
it seemed that summer was held in place.

John rose from the water
"Like a god," he said,
his arms outstretched, then lobbed the soap
grenade-like at my head.
It squirted past me, diving in the slips.

We dressed
– each stuck a dog-rose in his tunic –
and turned back to our trenches.
Pressed into the shadows, I thought:
What does this all mean?

Two young soldiers, for a moment
Sunday-school clean in all this mess.
The Taube crossed overhead, coughing smoke,
and made desperate way to his own lines.

Friedhof

They are tending the dead at Ypres.
The beech leaves, November bronze,
are lifted and rolled over
into rows between the slabs
by the gardener's blower
while three others follow to rake
the long mound and fork
this harvest into their barrows.

Behind the barbs of squared beech hedge
each yard of peace names its German dead,
twenty by twenty on dark, flat slabs
so that, without the steady sweepers,
you might come to this place as to a park,
tread the leaves in a path to the two figures
– a man, a woman; a father, a mother,
kneeling sharp and hunched before
some undetermined loss.

Years after the war, Käthe Kollwitz,
finding at last her only son's grave,
shaped these two from stone.
Now, his wooden cross a museum piece,
his name is flattened with the others
under this brief quilt of leaves.

At Tyne Cot, The New Irish Farm,
St Julien Dressing Station,
at Sanctuary Wood, at Lijssenthoek,
and a hundred cemeteries more,
the victorious dead, white-stoned, upright,

are ranked in the democracy of death –
Dorset, Welch, Highlander, Sikh,
Six men of the Chinese Labour Force.
The whole world bled through Flanders.

Turning the wet earth, Flemish farmers
still find wire and bones
tangled with the potatoes and beet.
And, occasionally, the local paper
carries at the bottom of a page –
Farmer blinded by shell.
It happens when they remove the detonator
from the rusty casing. The trade is well
established. The explosive is tired
but has a pedigree right enough for the men
of Armagh, Fermanagh, Crossmaglen.

Couples from the Fifties

Vague shapes stiff and grey all those miles away
The Coronation in our front-room – dull monotype, limited edition.

I smelt the Alvis's leather back seat as my father's radio declared
War on Egypt – the Suez route to India, East of Anthony Eden.

Mau Mau, Eoka, National Service, Singapore, Berlin.
The war won, the Empire dimming, the curtains coming down.

Rock 'n' Roll came to Carmarthen, two years late – the usherettes
Amazed as kids jived in the *Lyric's* aisles, just like the *Pathe News,*

Buddy, Elvis, Cliff, Gene, the original Comets and Bill.
The sweetest love-song ya ever heard – Don and Phil.

The outcasts, the lunch-time loners, the misunderstood,
We trekked to the lost geyser springs of Conti's espresso.

Coffee steam blends with Woodbine smoke and through it all
The Mekon juke-box doing slow-motion card tricks.

In Blackpool I held out my autograph book for David Nixon – in
        colour!
Who made playing cards machine-gun, vanish, then float back into
        view like gulls.

Dad's challenge – up the Lynton hill in the little black Austin, first
        gear:
Then back down on the brake to what the sea had left of the sea-wall,
        Lynmouth.

In the grey-dark matinees of the *Lyric* I plundered
The idea of oysters in a coral reef of petticoats.

Second Half

Three-nil down
and the wind to come
in our faces
for the second half.

The ball's barely
gone to hand –
we've kicked it
all away.

Warm scotch
in a cold, snug hipflask.
The sour end of the season
sweetens on the tongue.

My father would have
cheered and cheered
to make believe
in this match.

Next year, son,
big enough, you'll come
circled in my arms
from the crush.

We'll move into the crowd.
I'll learn to ease my hold.
Later, swept apart,
we'll spill out into the street

Taken for Pearls

In muddied waters the eyes of fishes
are taken for pearls.

As those two trout, little bigger than my hand then,
taken by spinner at Cresselly on an early

summer's day in the quiet afternoon
before the season's traffic. Only

a tractor in an unseen field
stitching the air like a canopy over it all.

And the taste of them pan-fried nose to tail
by my mother. The sweet flesh prised from

cages of the most skilfully carved bone.
I closed my eyes and she smiled for me.

At the Border

When I tilt the can over the herb border
she's planted, no water comes.
I tilt again, but still nothing shows.
Leaves, I suppose, have clogged
the spout from last autumn, rotted and plugged
so the water's locked in.

With both hands I lift to eye level
the laden, awkward can and tip again.
This roadside gift fallen from a builder's truck,
battered and cement-stained, with no rose,
has been ours for three different gardens. It won't work,
and I am miming in that silent film
where the children have stepped on the hose.

I lower it and shake, until from the sharp funnel
emerges like a pencil lead the beak
and then the head of a bird.
I make the water force it halfway through
until the shoulders clear and it thrusts
like some bow-sprit figure from the spout.
It is absurd and saddening – its eyes shut,
a blind, futile arrow.

One of this spring's young, curious,
has flown into the can's nesting dark
where I left it safe under the sycamores
and, soft thing, after its flutter
in the echoing space has chosen
that jewel of light promised at the spout
before the easy freedom of the can's wide brim.

Pointing its way up the shaft of blue sky
this days-old starling
wormed its way into a coffin of light
which tightened and starved it in the mildest of springs.
Now, in the early summer sun, I lift the can once more
and force the bird in a shower of wet light
out and into the herb border.

Safe from the magpies and neighbours' cats
in the musk of rosemary and marjoram,
worked by the weather, bone and feather
break down into soil that
feeds our parsley, chives and thyme.

Under the Yew

Gran, it's me. Passing through.
I've stopped again and bought these daffs for you.

No, it's the beginning of February.
They fly them in from somewhere now – Jersey,
abroad. They force them in greenhouses.
They're wiry and all the same
as if someone stamped them out on a machine,
but they'll last weeks
in the rain-water your urn's filled for them.
The cover had blown off with its dry sticks
of whatever they were I left last time
from the other side of Christmas. I've put it back.

I'm losing my feet, such terrible winds we have now.
That's all to do with greenhouses too,
but explaining would take more time than I've got,
Gran, and it's more than I really know.

The yew in front and to the left of you
is down like a drunk old man. The earth still
clings to its roots, out in the daylight
after god knows how many years. It fell
last week in the last gales, no doubt.
The one behind that overhangs your plot
has weathered firm enough. Shelter for years to come
and, I suppose, shade and shelter enough for my time.

There's blue sky, but not enough to patch a sleeve,
and the rain hammers down today like nails.
The Towy's up to the brim of the fields and about to spill.
At least driving home I'll go east before the weather.

It will be a month or two now, I expect
I come down to work, or just to see Mum.
Dad's so much dust on the coast path at Lydstep,
and that's nothing like the same.

I fly to America, Hong Kong, all over the place,
but the string is tied back here, as they say –
apron strings, heart strings, a way through the maze.

        The time. I have to go now.
The rain's coming hard again.
The motorway will be awash and dangerous as glass.
Everyone does such speed now, Gran.

Take care. And I'll take care.

Reg Webb

had sailed the five oceans
putting out from Cardiff, Singapore, Boston,
he'd cork-screwed merchantmen
through icy shoals of Atlantic U-boats, then
in peace, piloted the fat oil hulks through
the maze of the Haven's rocky green and blue,
with their confusion of pipes to nuzzle
and suckle the Milford terminals.

Reg, landlocked for years in an armchair
in front of the tv's babble, stared
at his chipboard fire-place, the china,
chintz and brass, the gaudy gilt mirror.
Awash with bile, incontinent, bilges leaking,
his eyes watery and vast, was past pottering
with the roses and bulbs of the flat's
flower border, and shooing away cats.

Reg, becalmed in the straits of morphine
captaining his bed, full-sheeted, trim,
away from the port of his front room and tv,
the photo at the Palace for his O.B.E.
floundering and sick of being ill,
sank angrily, far out in the cottage hospital.
He's lost now, with fire in the hold, and a hard stoke
for one last evasive action, making smoke.

The Captain's Diary

1909. On the whole, a good year. By chance
the summer has left the grass full and strong
after our uncommonly late winter.
The new half of nine holes is settling down,
though the greens will, no doubt, need years longer.
Rabbits continue to create a damn nuisance;
the professional has borrowed a shotgun.

We have resolved at last, with common sense,
the issue of the women. Surely it is bad
enough encountering them on the course without ceding
government of the Tenby club to them. The ladies,
some of them, may play decently enough, but having
their own captain and secretary gives them
all the say they need without hampering
the business of the club with their chatter and whinge.
Now they have Miss Adela Voyle, if you please,
as their "Captain" and the trappings of their own club.
All this won without platform, chains or a food syringe!

A greater number of visitors this summer.
Caught one fellow using a cleek – a cleek!
– off the seventh tee. *Use your driver, sir!*
A driver, if you please. I sent him packing
and will keep an eye out for him in future.
These visitors contribute to the revenue lacking
but nothing justifies such impertinent cheek.

High tides will prove a problem should we persist
with those holes along the South Beach
for that fine prospect of Caldey Island and the coast.
The Rev. Morris proclaims that if God had
meant there to be a golf course here then He
would have marked one out. Sometimes Morris has a manner
too flip for the propriety of his calling.
(I answered him with a belch.
We were at the sherry decanter, be it said.)
Though our most celebrated guest seemed to welcome
that sort of banter. His Majesty's Chancellor
proved to be a passable hitter of the ball,
though prone to take in the view too much
to consider seriously the challenge of the golfing.
It is said he will cut a road
in the history of our empire. Certainly,
it is held to be a matter of note for the Welsh
that one of their number be counted in such office.

He is of no great height for a man of coming greatness
and his eyes dart at times like a goat's,
not wishing to miss one moment. Except on a tee,
I am thinking here of the Black Rock from which, as I say,
his gaze was something of a dreamer's.
"The land", he said, (and all the time,
to my intense irritation, he called me 'Doctor M')
it is as if a giant had scooped the grass and sand.
Or great engines of war had gouged the earth in bites,
that now grows back to heal its wounds."
Which I thought smacked too fully of the poet
and too little of the real man.
Though, in truth, there were rifle cracklings aplenty
as we passed the Lifter's Cottage, playing the Railway
and holes through the Penally Butts.

It is my belief that we have recovered completely,
as a body of sportsmen, if not in our fiscal health,
from the loss of that land to the Army.
What seemed indeed a hard blow four years ago when all
our efforts to build an 18-hole course were washed away
as surely as if the sea rose over us in storm,
we have now had to put behind us. The Army's needs etcetera...
Though Mr Lloyd George seemed not inclined to deal
with this German Navy business when the vicar,
that fool Morris, raised it at dinner.
For my part, I think the Powers shall resolve matters
as good managers ought with the world's affairs.
God preserve us from another engagement. The Boers...
These riflemen on the ranges at Penally are like golfers
at their practice. In readiness for the game.

The Tradesmen's Club issue has now been resolved.
I for one see little harm, provided their play
is restricted. They will prove useful in maintenance work.
However, the trial of the early closing day
free golf for the shop-keeping class could open up doors
best left closed. A course supervised by James Braid,
Champion of the British Isles, must needs be strictly governed.
It was my honour to partner Braid in a medal fours.

Morris has word that Mathias-Thomas has bought the four holes
belonging to Davies's land. I think this bodes ill,
for while Lord Davies of Llandinam has much
to occupy himself with his empire of coals,
(not to mention Lloyd George's tilt at the Upper House)
Mathias-Thomas will surely look to catch a profit
from his acquisition. At the least, my land –
the marshes up to Black Pool – is secure yet,
and could, if needed, bring some three further

holes into play. This land business,
and the continuing pressure for Sunday golf
darkens further the prospect of the impending winter.
Already the mornings are chill and the wind
from the Irish Sea cuts through tweed like a bayonet.

Queen's Tears

In ten years, not once have these colours shown.
Inherited with our house
then relegated to my college room,
its dull green-margined petals
have filled my window space for two years.
And now *Billbergia Windii*, Queen's Tears
sends five tendrils out with five pink sepals,
each unclenching a pendant of flowers,
blue and yellow and red.

I inherited the room, too. David
tall and balding, fiftyish, worked here –
incongruous suit and acting pumps,
an English voice that could be powerful or plum.
It's four years since he died. A Fulbright
to California did for him –
long afternoons cruising for lovers in the sun,
anonymous bath-house couplings at night.

He sat in the office as they phoned the doctor.
I saw him there, shaking with the sweats,
his slack mouth caked with saliva.
His mind had gone beyond us. Staring ahead
he knew what was plain for us to see.

He had no family. At the funeral, actress
friends from his drama school days
did something from Proust, a Donne sonnet
beautifully read, to an audience
of colleagues and dutiful boss.

Another spring is due, the magnolia tree
knocks against the window. My first floor
view frames an angle of buildings
and the sky's parade of clouds behind
the failing *Queen's Tears*.

David, let the deep green, loud red
and ice blue sing for you
and all the casual folk I never really knew,
but think of on occasions, remotely, from the past,
as now. Brief flowerings that come
unannounced, and do not last.

Summer in Bangkok

The second day he bought a wife
for his stay.
He kept her in his room and fucked
her all the ways he'd ever dreamed.
She was fed and kept
and smiled and answered his needs.

It was perfect, save that her English
was a dozen, broken sentences.

Some days he would go to see the city:
then she ran herself clean under the shower,
she moved around the room trailing her hand
over polished wood, curtains, picture frames.
She lay on the bed he tied her to.

And in the final week he took the interior trek
– eight guys led into the hills
and poisonous snakes, bare-teeth monkeys.
They burned leeches from their arms and legs.
In the trees were men with guns and heroin eyes.
Their women were invisible, their children sold to the city.

Each night he shivered. They were locked
in by the massive dark, a wall of sounds.
Like children they went to piss in pairs.
When he looked up the sky was small. He saw
no plough, no bear, no hunter.
The stars would not be read.

On the fourth day they struck the river and turned,
made bamboo rafts with poles and rode the white water
back to the coast, the skyscrapers, the wild taxis,
the silk, the child beggars, career amputees.

Halfway, they poled a long, slow curve and met
the heroin men on both banks, rifles raised
and aimed at them. Their guide spoke loudly
and quickly, his hands eloquent, then fevered,
the rest kept still on the bobbing water.
He gripped his pole tightly, all he could do,
so it stuck and trembled in the river bottom.
He had no words.

Back on the hotel she lay on his bed,
her hair spread wet on his pillow, her arms
and legs, as it were, swimming.

Brady's Glass

The senator's wife herself served us – tossed
fresh salad with the finest ham:
full cured Virginia, at god knows what cost,
the tomatoes somewhat underripe, but fat.

Our conversation turned to the war
– Lee's retreat and his scorching of the South –
until a crash of glass brought Silus
and the other boy to the door.

His barrow had tipped against the glasshouse, splinters
were scattered like ice all around. "Brady's glass,"
the Senator said, "his photographist's pictures
from Antietam, when we held against Jackson.

The dead at Sharpsburg, at the Bloody Lane –
most distressing. The public's sense of shock
was very regrettable. The plates he left
were just the size for hot house panes."

Silus fitted fresh glass from a stock
he kept in the stables. Faint grey ghosts fallen
in a dirt road ditch with awkward limbs
and bloated bellies, backs arched in pain.

All that summer the sun shone through
those stiffened dead, printing them
on to the green leaves and ripening crop,
bruises in the fruit that were grey and blue.

From the hills, the town

As he talks he rolls an apple in his hands
which with the force of his thumbs
he splits to make two glistening
full-waxed moons of sweet flesh.
Below, the town is a mouth of broken teeth.
In his mind it is geometry, lines form a grid
– the runway, the mosques, the bread shops.
His face is a map of the long year.

Stones and mortars. But now it is a quiet time.
Though the day still has warmth, his men huddle
around a stove, the smoke of bacon, coffee.
Suddenly hungry, his eyes blink wide.
He fits the two apple halves back together
and bites from one, then the other.

Incident on a hospital train
from Calcutta, 1944

At a water-stop three hours out
the dry wail of brakes ground us down
from constant jolting pain to an oven
heat that filled with moans and shouts
from wards the length of six carriages.

We had pulled slowly up towards the summer
hills for coolness. They were hours distant,
hazy and vague. I opened the grimy
window to a rush of heat
and, wrapped in sacking, a baby

held up like some cooked offering from its mother –
Memsahib...meri buchee ko bachalo...Memsahib take –
pushed like an unlooked-for gift into my arms.
She turned into the smoke and steam.
I never saw her face.

As we lumbered off I unwrapped
a dirty, days-old girl, too weak for cries.
Her bird weight and fever-filled eyes
already put her out of our reach. By Murree Junction
that child would have emptied half our beds.

At the next water-stop my nurses left her.
The corporal whose arms had gone looked up at me
and said, *There was nothing else to do.*
Gangrenous, he died at Murree a week later.
His eyes, I remember, were clear, deep and blue.

The Night-trees

Again in the ninth month
he takes his spade to the field.

This is in the late evening
when the darkness is down
and his neighbours indoors.

Slowly he digs a hole –
a tree for a boy: for a girl, a grave.
And this is the fifth time.

He sits there on the broken ground
until the village lights go out
and the fires die. Until
the sun shapes the morning hills.

She has worked all evening at a blanket,
resting it on her stomach.
All night she lies listening.
The hole is out of hearing.

Then each night until her time
she wakes early and in the heavy dark
listens for wind, the rustle of leaves
from his three trees

or the night-birds flying
to perch there with the soft sounds
girls might whisper
one to the other.

Portrait of the Painter Hans Theo Richter and his wife Gisela in Dresden, 1933

This is the perfect moment of love –
Her arm around his neck,
Holding a rose.

Her wisps of yellow hair
The light turns gold.
Her face is the moon to his earth.

Otto's studio wall glows
With the warm wheat glow
Of the loving couple.

This is after the dark etchings,
The blown faces. This is after Bapaume –
The sickly greens, the fallen browns.

She is a tree, her neck a swan's curved to him.
His hands enclose her left hand
Like folded wings.

This is before the fire-storm,
Before the black wind,
The city turned to broken teeth.

It is she who holds the rose to him,
Theo's eyes which lower in contentment
To the surgeon's smock he wears for painting.

This is the perfect moment,
The painted moment
She will not survive.

This is before the hair that flames,
The face that chars. This is before
Her long arms blacken like winter boughs.

This is the harvest of their love,
It is summer in the soul,
The moment they have made together.

From Otto's window the sounds of the day –
The baker's boy calling, a neighbour's wireless
playing marches and then a speech.

The Visit to Terezin

Here are the houses.
There is a light there, and listen
– someone sings.
How clean the streets, yes?
A tidy people, we have observed,
with their own pride.

Here is their bakery and, do you see,
a cobbler, carpenter, the butcher
with their own beliefs
in the killing for meat.
We come to the school. Later we will
be entertained by their orchestra.
A race is redeemed by music, I think.

Look at the children's pictures. You see –
houses with fences. The chimneys smoke
– there are families inside.
A giant – look at his club, his boots.
Where there are children, there will be giants.
And always butterflies, look, so many colours,
they use all the colours,
as large as kites, as large as clouds.
Where a child's mind flies, yes?
This one has played the gallows game.
Or it could be a door.

The bowl and the spoon

Behind the high wire
In a hut under the stilted towers
two women face each other.
Between them a wooden bowl and a spoon.

Each in turn takes the spoon.
They hold the bowl with care,
like a rare porcelain, firm,
concentrating the eyes, the fingers.

A spoonful, a spoonful,
another dry swallow
so that still the bowl
holds its same level of soup.

After a while and without words
the daughter at her turn lifts
a spoonful away from her dry mouth
and puts it to her mother's.

She takes the soup, then with her turn
feeds her daughter. In this way
the bowl is tilted and emptied,
only in this way is the spoon licked dry.

A full moon has risen through the wire
like a cut cheese. Light
cat-licks the bowl and spoon
on the bare table.

In this world this is the love we make –
to the strongest the food,
the life to come. Our only grail
an empty spoon.

Sutherland at Picton Ferry

At his back
the salt-sour murmur of the tide,
the rustle and crackle of reeds
at that moment they change
supple green to starched yellow.

At his back the woods and garden's purple and pinks,
azaleas, rhododendrons,
clutches of brief colour in the early Summer sun.
In Wales they grow in masses on the old-money estates
like weeds for the crach-ach.

The curl-ee, curl-ee, curl-ee,
then the bird climbs into the air
to skim over the river, a single letter
written against the far bank, down the eastern Cleddau
into a freshening breeze off the sea that moves
the reeds, the leaves, the water and clouds
at his back, unseen but necessary
to the roots he stares at so the looking,
because of the otherness of all these things,
changes what is looked at,
and the roots define the hollows and shades
brown earth has caught
in the convolutions of space in the form.
And then there is no river, no sky
no curlew's cry, no reeds, no Pembrokeshire,
but shapes and space only.

He peers at the form, in below the great bole
of the tree rampant above him as a leopard's head
– blunt with eyes and the line of a mouth –
and the roots are sinews of a neck,
the muscles and ligaments of a strength
held in the bank, displayed
by the tide's scalpel.

He looks and looks until
the earth, the tree, the salt smell of the estuary
fold into pure form and become
torso, cave, grave, cruciform.

Coracle

Sea Oracle –
wattled water rider, sewin slayer,
Towy tossed when the tide rises.
Man-shell – two tortoises
crawling from the falling sun,
or the wings of a black moth.
Two halves of a cockleshell
drifting back to a whloe.

One arm twisting like ivy
round the smooth paddle
to stir the water like thick cawl,
the other weighing the net's haul
from its slow semi-circle of river-trawl.
And then the unstrapped truncheon,
brought down for the sharp crack of bone,
the last slap of dispatch.

Thimbles worn against
the current's sharpening point
with their slung-between fish pen,
gill-snagging, fin-trapping,
cow hair spun into strings
that play the deep song of the river.
The catch of silver
in the midas touch of moonlight.

William Orpen & Yvonne Aubicq
in the Rue Dannon

This morning he wakes early –
sun and the sounds of carts in the streets
coming through the roughly-drawn curtains,
a fine March light over the city.
She has lain an arm across his shoulder.
In sleep her beauty is muted, held somewhere
ringing like the glint of a far-off bell.
He has seen them in ruins, the churches,
the chateaux, the empty, crumbling town squares.
He has coloured them green against brown,
yellow against dirt, the torn bodies,
the green limbs under shell-hole water.
He dreamt of lobsters moving behind glass
in the restaurant at the Savoy.
Yvonne stirs under his breath,
her sleeping face turns halfway to his.
The head is perfect under night-tousled hair,
her eyelids shimmer like butterflies' wings.
There is painting and life and death.
The mayor's beautiful daughter lies in his bed.
He is having a good war.

Last August baked the mud of the Somme
into a pure, dazzling white. And there
were daisies, blood-red poppies
and a blue flower, for miles it seemed,
great masses of blue that were,
close-to, particular delicacies.
The sky a pure, dark blue and the whole air
for thirty feet up or more quivered
with white butterflies. I brushed them – I was gentle – from
my uniform as I returned to the car.
We drove on through fields of white crosses,
the butterflies slamming against my driver's glass
as if those crosses lurched out of the unsettled earth.

At Thiepval I began to paint a trench.
It held the remnants of two soldiers
– one German, one of ours..

I could not hold the sight for too long at a time
so gave myself rest against the torn trunk of a tree.
Three sessions, an hour passed, and then
a loose shell came over and burst.

I was blown backwards head over arse.
My heavy portrait easel took the force
– a skull smashed up through the canvas –
and the whole scene was blown to hell.

He slips away from her embrace
and she murmurs in sleep.
Tomorrow or the next day it will be complete –
the light on that slope of her left shoulder,
more work on the hair perhaps. He'll
watch her comb it as he loads his palette.
He has caught her classically
holding herself back from one's gaze,
arms crossed over her breasts
Pulling her robe to her right shoulder,
That teasing look will devastate.

He rises, wraps the robe about himself
and crosses to the window to light a cigarette.
From the balcony he blows smoke over Paris.

At the end of the Rue Dannon is a square.
This is where they will march her — yes
I'll say she is a spy — call her Frida Neiter —
a spy for the Boche that the French will shoot.
She does not scream or struggle,
but walks upright, across the road
to the wall.
As the soldiers raise their rifles and
the officer his sword, she lets
slip her fur coat to the ground.
Naked she stands to face them,
her arms held out from her sides.

It seems a lifetime before they fire.

The Front

He took a bullet
and fell.
I went down to him
ducked under their fire.

I have you
It's alright
I said.

Pulling his arms around my neck
I carried him back
to the safety of our line.
His face was wet against my neck.

They did not let up
the whole way.

Taking bullets all the while
he died against me
and I wore him
like a pelt
my shield
my brother
my other skin.

The Death of Richard Beattie-Seaman in the Belgian Grand Prix, 1939

Trapped in the wreckage by his broken arm
he watched the flames flower from the front end.
So much pain – Holy Jesus, let them get to me –
so much pain he heard his screams like music
when he closed his eyes – the school organ at Rugby,
Matins with light slanting down
hot and heady from the summer's high windows.
Pain – his trousers welded by flame to his legs.
His left hand tore off the clouded goggles –
rain falling like light into the heavy trees,
the track polished like a blade.
They would get to him, they were all coming
all running across the grass, he knew.

The fumes of a tuned Mercedes smelt like
boot polish and tear gas – coughing, his screams rising
high out of the cockpit – high
away back to '38 Die Nurburgring.
He flew in with Clara
banking and turning the Wessex through a slow circle
over the scene – sunlight flashing off the line of cars,
people waving, hoardings and loudspeakers, swastikas
and the flags of nations lifted in the wind he stirred.
She held his arm tightly, her eyes were closed.
He felt strong like the stretched wing of a bird,
the course mapped out below him.
That day Lang and Von Brauchitsch and Caracciola
all dropped out and he did it – won
in the fourth Mercedes before a crowd of half a million
– the champagne cup, the wreath around his neck,
An Englishman the toast of Germany
The camera caught him giving a Hitlergruss.

Waving arms, shouts and faces, a mosaic
laid up to this moment – La Source – tight – the hairpin
in the trees – tight – La Source – keeping up the pace
Belgium – La Source hairpin too tight.
With the fire dying, the pain dying,
the voices blurred beneath the cool licks of rain.
To be laid under the cool sheets of rain.
A quiet with, just perceptible, engines roaring
as at the start of a great race.

Home Front

That winter of our Island Fortress,
the docks blacked-out and sirens wailing,
the house closed its brittle silence around her.
Rain drummed the windows behind her children's dreams.
Over the months she saved from her widow's pay
and the hours of cleaning at the manse
seven silver coins, one from the abdication year
with the head of the love-lost king.

Should the coastline be split by incoming shells,
parachutes flower in the Vale
and jackboots strut in King's Square,
then she would lay her six children
to sleep, sealing the windows and doors
with newspapers and blankets.
Seven shillings' worth of gas
would deliver them out of occupation.

For months she has dreamt of his lost freighter,
torpedoed six days out of New York,
men overboard, gagging on salt and diesel.
How the ship reared and plunged like a whale,
her wash sweeping cold hands from flotsam.
As he sank into the anonymous dark
the final waves from her
minting coins from the constant moon.

Tonight the City of London burns
with St Paul's untouched at the very centre.
At the edge of night the Welsh ports sound no alarms.
She opens the curtains to a moon-bright sky,
counts out the coins in the tea-caddy
and holds them, cupped in her palms.
OMN. REX. Defender of the faith. Emperor of India.
The seven polished shillings sing in her hands.

Poles

An ancient woman in black
bends slowly over her row of beans.
The crop has come and gone and now
she pulls the yellow plants in bunches
out of the earth. She loosens
each pole of the row, then stretches to pull
the cross-stick which secures the length.
She works inch by inch,
a black shape against the shadows of the trees
and the whiteness of her ducks.
Passing down the road – Panzers, *Coca-Cola* trucks,
coaches of tourists. Beyond her plot
the sea in which we swim, from which we run
exhausted, tingling with salt, laughing.
Now she has raised the centre stick.
It balances on her finger tips like a javelin.
She lays it on the sheaf of spent poles
as they did at Thermopylae.

Lines at Barry

Morning light steely and sharp on the docks-water
and beyond, outlining a ship in the grey Channel.
At berth, one banana ship white against the old mill building
where, you say, a forest of masts grew in the sun,
filling your great-grandfather's vision
as he rounded Friar's Point.

Ten days rowing from Fishguard
the length of South Wales. 1898.
Your grandmother lived her first week
in that small boat as they hugged the shore,
sheltering each night where lights marked
fire and food and life.

This is not a unique story:
each dip of his creaking blades pulling
towards coal, English and the new century.

Twenty years on he was carpenter to the town,
settled and secure in his middle life.
They'd worked all night to build a platform
for the notables, under the Stars and Stripes,
the Red Dragon, the Union Jack.
The next day he took his place in the crowd
around King's Square and stretched for a view.
This is where the Yanks first came in,
eight days rolled across the ocean
then marched in columns up from the packed, grey harbour.
The doughboys formed in dress order,
spreading and flexing their sea-legs,
the men bound in puttees, their officers' boots glowing,
the strange, stiff-brimmed campaign hats,
lines of polished Springfields raised against the Kaiser.

And for a moment between the speeches,
the cheering, the singing and the drill,
for a moment the lines were still and erect
as those distant masts had been for a moment still,
when the only sound was the sound of the tide pulling
his tiny boat: he saw again Sarah's tired smile,

the baby pressed to her nipple and sucking,
sucking hard, as if nothing else, not even he, existed.
As this new morning goes, the haze
lifts slowly from the Channel, unveils
the munitions ship with her red flags up
and lighters packed with shells
drawing lines of foam to the smack centre of her sides.

Three lifetimes, two wars running to this moment –
and none of this is unique, this telling,
this drawing from memory of lines
where, steely-silver, what we are now
touches everything that made us,
and is dangerous, and shines.

Lessons

Right up the edge of the pit
The Professor of History taught:

Every tree, every cry
Every tear, every leaf
Each death, each blade
Of grass. Remember everything!
We are scribes – one of us
Perhaps will survive
And be all our future.

The wet, black earth on our feet.
The rattle of bullets in the trees.
The sun jewelling that belt-buckle.

At Birkenau I saw one of your kind –
He was in the Sonderkommando at the crematoria
Scribbling lists by the light of the furnaces.
I snapped the pencil and tore the paper –
He said nothing.
We made him throw open the doors and put them in –

He was silent.
Then we shot him and fed him to the flames.
On my walk back to the barracks
I read his name in the sky.

Soup

One night our block leader set a competition:
two bowls of soup to the best teller of a tale.
That whole evening the hut filled with words –
tales from the old countries
of wolves and children
potions and love-sick herders
stupid woodsmen and crafty villagers.
Apple-blossom snowed from blue skies,
orphans discovered themselves royal.
Tales of greed and heroes and cunning survival,
soldiers of the Empires, the Church, the Reich.

And when they turned to me
I could not speak,
sunk in the horror of that place,
my throat a corridor of bones, my eyes
and nostrils clogged with self-pity.
'Speak,' they said, 'everyone has a story to tell.'
And so I closed my eyes and said:
I have no hunger for your bowls of soup, you see
I have just risen from the Shabbat meal –
my father has filled our glasses with wine,
bread has been broken, the maid has served fish.
Grandfather has sung, tears in his eyes, the old songs.
My mother holds her glass by the stem, lifts
it to her mouth, the red glow reflecting on her throat.
I go to her side and she kisses me for bed.
My grandfather's kiss is rough and soft like an apricot.
The sheets on my bed are crisp and flat
like the leaves of a book ...

I carried my prizes back to my bunk: one bowl
I hid, the other I stirred
and smelt a long time, so long
that it filled the cauldron of my head,
drowning a family of memories.

The Grammar

They were never dull, those half-remembered,
half-composed men, our masters.

We joined with them in some conspiracy
(the grey-trousered 'Fifties needed authority)

and the hurts they did us dull down the years,
those classroom NCO's from some distant war of tears.

Some had survived, like Jenkins Chem whose face
was one big scar from when his tank bought it at Falaise.

Others missed the show, or dodged the chance to fight:
they lived through peacetime's sterile wank.

Perhaps they took it out on us, the celebration
fruit of victory over Hitler and the Japs; a generation

not long enough on the branch, fallen,
rotten on coffee and juke-box rock'n'roll.

We made them the stuff of boyhood myth, and all
colluded in that corridored game they played.

We had the hatred of all arty things
an all-male institution brings:

Roberts Music played us Chopin, the poof,
but set us shivering with that Mussorgsky stuff.

Ethy the Art taught us nothing at all. Smutty
Michaelangeloes, we'd draw in his David's classical balls

and rather die than meet him behind the board
– hands on flies, backs to the wall.

Maths when Bonzo Davies would chalk backwards on a dap
BONZO – and print it on your bum with a public wack.

And all the time the skirmishings ran on:
their job to keep us under the thumb;

our skill in changing words of the hymns
and silent, riotous farting in the assembly hall gyms.

Then stinging ears, arse canings.
A system of rude awakenings.

Those well-remembered, rarely-composed men, our masters,
coloured in our formative years, the clever bastards.

At Ochrid Lake

for Zoran Anchevski

After the monastery of Sveta Naum,
after the frescoes and the blank spaces
of the stolen frescoes,
after the poems and cameras
and the sound-crew man who played for us
James Taylor on his guitar, we swim
beneath the mountains
in the lake's shallow warmth,
feet curling over the smooth, muddy pebbles.

Around the headland Albania's
border-posts, visa checks, the guard's cold eyes.
Across the lake are the blue-distant Greek hills.
Macedonia wedged into the Balkans –
tyrannized, subjugated, partitioned
by Greeks, Serbs, Bulgars, Turks, Nazis,
the Austro-Hungarian Empire,
century after century.

Zoran, once you climbed in these mountains
to find still the scars of the Great War –
shallow trenches cut into the rocks,
brambles of wire, shells, skulls
bleached white like great birds' eggs.

Beneath the hills
from the shadowed groves at our backs
pure water springs from the ground,
gathers into a river that courses
a current clear through the lake.

As we wade from the shallows
further into the flow, the river hits
us like a wall of cold. Suddenly
icy the water's caress turns
to manacles locked around our legs –
it is like the promise of death, then
under this faultless sky,
like death itself.

Great Uncle Charlie

1893-1980

What better way to end it all
than this January day,
the fields across to Peasmore fresh with rain
and Enbourne's church, St Michael
and All Angels, held in seven centuries of air;
the grave's sides of polished Berkshire clay?

Now the month-old holly lies in our hearth,
spikes curled and brown,
but the berries' fire still glows
red as the poppy in his wreath.

The last time we saw him alive,
a week before Christmas,
was in the cottage hospital flanked
by two of the dying, the obviously dying,
his mouth slack and eyes closed,
until our voices woke him
and he smiled. His eyes brightened
and widened under the full, white head of hair.
He shook our hands, that odd
grip with two finger-ends lost
in the press at Simpson's the printers
where he'd been apprenticed as a lad.
Pronounced unfit with a dicky heart
for Haig's trenches, he'd lived
to see this century to its last gasp.

For an hour and a half he kept us talking,
flirting with a nurse, joking with the tea-lady.
Then I brought him round to the war:
They chose me from the ambulance men
and had me dressed in full uniform
to drive the old King to Reading,
to the station where they brought the wounded in.
Rows and rows of stretchers along the platform.
And a band playing full blast.
Old George, he stopped every yard or so,
and some of'em (and here Charlie lowered his voice

in deference to those dying at his sides)
had no ... (he touched his arm) *and some of'em*
no (and here his leg). *An'you know*
what his majesty said – he said, Don't
you worry my man (and most of'em were
no more than boys) don't you worry he said,
we shall soon have you back and fighting the Hun.'
Charlie's eyes focussed away to the far wall.
One morning Mrs Cooper at Thatcham
lost all three of her sons.
Same morning.
On the Somme.

Before driving back we took
armfuls of ripe holly from his tree
at the backdoor.
                    D'you know
how that tree came to be here?
One day I left my spade in the earth
and a robin perched there.

That holly was no higher than myself
and just out of shot as we posed for family snaps
– Uncle and Dad and Mum and Gran and me
pulling at my slack bow and arrow.
My father's jacket bulging with coins,
keys, tobacco, just like Charlie's,
his hand gripping a pipe, the other
clenched in his pocket, just like Charlie's.

Great Uncle Charlie,
you survive all the characters.
I place you at the wheel of a Ford Pop,
chugging to the top of the Air-Balloon.
Perched on that hill like a climber
looking back towards Berkshire,
you're rubbing tobacco in your palm,
packing it down in the bowl as if those finger
-stumps had been fashioned for the act.

The match flares for a moment
and the smoke catches in a wind that
twists it up and over your face. From below
it seems, almost, a halo.

In McDonough County

for Fred and Nancy Jones

Waiting for you this morning
alone and chilled in the empty house
I walked out, crossing the road and ditch to the fields.
Miles of corn, October brown rising
firm out of the black earth.

As far as the sky it stretched
and what I had taken for a block of colour, a mass
of uniform growth, showed itself particular, alive –
the electric whine of crickets, their clicked-finger jumps,
a fox, a racoon, crashing through the lines.
The corn moves in the prairie breeze,
stalks and drooping leaves that scratch
and tap against each other – the whole landscape
like the flaking skin and bristles of this world.

The sky was wider than the eye could hold –
blue with a light hand of cloud below
the high streaks of jet planes.
I felt into the hanging pods
to the smooth, full barrels of maize.

Now, at uneasy midnight, I am woken
by a low, wide rumbling – lights spark
and turn out there in the blackness.
They are working through the night
to beat the threat of rain – combines
chewing down the rows, ruling the farms' geometry.
In the damp morning light their chutes
will pour rich fountains, gold atoms
splashing into the trucks.

Dakota, Nebraska, Illinois, Iowa, Ohio –
across this vast Mid-West
the grain silos rise like cased Havanas
blunt, silver missiles.
On a high-nineties August day, without warning,
you say, one explodes.

The Arches

Poems in respone to the collages of John Digby

I

There are always two ways
of looking at a thing.

Botticelli the lighthouse keeper
stares over the rocks' spume and flash
until the crash of waves
curl to form a shell
she grows from.
Modest, voluptuous tresses
folded around her.

The gulls, the bawdy gulls
screech in the angry, randy air.

Inside, the other man
does all he can
to placate the raucous sea.
He has thrown amphorae
to the waves.
        'What do you want?
What am I to do?'
he calls.

With his knife
he has sliced away one skin, one face.
New, young again, he feels strong,
strong enough to jump through the rough arch,
through the mirage of her
and strike out for the lighthouse,
the attainable lighthouse.

VIII

Under the sickle moon
I shall be Alice
and follow the svelte rabbit
out of the ruined tower
passing to the arch where, huge,
I find the medicine and spoon.

A spoonful, a spoonful.
It would be so easy here
and now, the stars at my back,
the rustling trees with their advice,
the moon a slice of used light.

The music of leaves washes through me.
I know that there is something immense
I must do. Something.

There is a device on the handle of the spoon
that the craftsman has cleverly engraved.
An apple ripe on the branch
which a hand should close around.

XVII

This was not meant to be.
I thought that we were on lines
to some kind of place together,
some heights we both could see.

But there, like a mammoth,
was the tusked imperative of common sense.
Derailed, a tangled mess, I felt upended.
And then we stopped using words.

Into the icy quiet of our aftermath,
only the sound of your chair creaking
as you bent to pick up the pieces
of a broken coffee cup.

XX

Mama and I went behind the arches
to change me for the bathing.
'There,' she said, 'Be gone!'
to the excited birds that wheeled
before us as if sensing food.

She had smoothed oil on me
against the sun and wind
and the salt of the sea.

I saw only flying boy-hungry creatures
from the beginnings of time
that smelling my oiled body
were tasting me with their wet eyes.

The moon strangely in the same sky
as the low sun
grew large and like some huge stone
began to roll towards us, quite filling the sky.

'Hold me, Mama!' I cried,
though uttered not a word
that she could hear, 'Hold me
against the moon,
against all the creatures of the sky.
Against the salty hunger of the sea.'

XXII

High in the peaks
above the snowline
has appeared a tower
from which a prophet calls.
His outstretched arms are reaching for the world.

Here the prayers are pure and principled
in the rare and clean air,
though the words travel
like knives down over the snow,
the lichened rocks, the grazing slopes,
over the desert to the seas
where, in time, whales beach themselves
helplessly, knowing no reason.

This was ever the way –
from the high clarity
the waves of confusion
turn to the words
that lead us astray.

XXIII

After the dwarf gladiators,
the bladed chariot races,
the monkey crucifixion,
today the Emperor puts on
the spotted horse.

From the four corners
of the greatest empire
the world will ever know
new wonders are brought for our show.

The armoured bull.
The white deer and the pink.
The giant cats that tame men.

And now the spotted horse
is slung into the arena –
its spindle legs akimbo,
its stretched neck, nose
balancing an amphora full,
it is said, with myrrh,
spice, frankincense,
it would take a man
his life to earn.

Oh, and we gasp,
we cry. Everything
is in the balance.

Heaven's Gate

for Dannie and Joan Abse

Outside the Mughal Emperor in the sharp air
under a sky precise as a map
we point at Hale Bopp and its final, slow
splash out of our world into the depthless dark.
Full up with lamb pasanda, chicken jalfrezi
and puffed, sweet naan, we couldn't be
more earth-bound, more remote from flight.

There they go,
the thirty-three California crazies
who gave up on our century.
They're dead as dodos sailing through heaven's gate
in the gas stream of the comet
with their personal guides, the aliens.

While we, full of wind and spice, look
up from the jammed tight car park,
without envy or scorn,
but warm in friendship and food
and the pleasure of living this night
six million by six million miles below
the chaos of the gas and rock that now,
just now, completes this perfect sky
with a painter's smear of titanium white.

Icarus

Out of an English summer morning's sky
drops an Indian who failed in flight
miles short of heaven. This frozen Icarus
thrown from the wheel-bay of a 747
splashes into a Surrey reservoir,
cracking the water like a whip.

This poor man stowed away
in the Delhi heat, curled
himself into an oven of rubber and oil,
and dreamed as he rose in the deafening take-off
of food and rain and Coca Cola
and television where the colour never ends.

The waitress at the Granada stop
tapping in two coffees and a Danish
at the till, for no reason at all,
looked up, saw a bird, or an engine,
or a man, and then nothing
but blue sky again.

Blackberries at Pwllcrochan

I drive through Rhoscrowther, through rain.
The refinery has dwarfed the village –
two dozen houses, the church and its graves
under the lea of the hill.
Oil buys out the houses, one by one,
boarded up and numbered for demolition,
as death, job, despair or the money pushes people out.

Those miles of Texaco pipes, barbed fence,
it all goes out of sight as I turn back
down the tunnelled lane to Pwllcrochan –
the church deconsecrated,
boarded-up school and bricked-blind house.
I pull in beside the flattened Rectory's ground
as the security jeep passes by on its round.

The stone barn seems smaller now, and where
that tangled bank of blackberries thicken,
there was the old Rectory, my uncle's. I remember it
huge, too big to fit this space. Here
the kitchen, with its cosy, constant Aga,
potatoes fresh from their fields rattling in the pan,
warm milk and roasted, earthy chickens.
My auntie gave suck at that table,
her great breast singled like a moon.

This is one of the places it begins,
the diaspora of feelings.

Under this pressed earth, was the cellar –
stacked seed potatoes, wrinkled, their eyes on stalks,
and the oily generator my father drove us down for,
weekends of tinkering, conjuring the pulsing light.
And there, higher than that sycamore,

the bedrooms where my cousins and I were tucked
in for the long, name-calling, tumbling nights.
In the disappeared orchard
we climbed and swung for apples;
we forked at rats in the barn's back stores.

Now and here it starts,
the weighing of the heart.

The rain chills my face and neck.
It sweeps from the west, blearing the hard
gleam of the massive pipes and tanks
where Bummer George's wood has been sliced
out of the land. The wet gusts carry
the dull, metalled workings of the refinery.

I start to pick the plump, washed, blackberries.
In my cupped hands they have the weight
of blown birds' eggs, and their seedy,
sweet music plays in the mouth.

Ernie's House

Ernest Zobole: "The later perspective is a tyranny."

There is always the man
in the house
with his easel.

His wife and dog are also in the house
but may not always be seen.

The house looks over a valley
down which the river slides
to the sea.

It has been coal-black and bitter,
but now salmon muscle against its blue-black flow.

The valley is terraced with houses
that are growing empty.

The hills hunch their shoulders
and wait to be counted.

More often than not it is
night. Stars. More stars.

The lights of cars explode,
the street-lamps come into bloom.
The graveyard's crosses glint.

Far off, at sea, ships
on their way to everywhere else.

Lottie Stafford's neck

Morning sunlight catching
the heat of her like sex.
The way the light glazes her neck
at that moment she turns,
her hands gripping the washing tub,
as Jenny comes down the stairs with
the bedding across her shoulders
in a fluster of gossip.

That shining, taut slope of skin
Sir William caught with his brushes,
a scene from the mind,
the life of service he imagined.
Hours in his studio after work
her neck craned and stiffening
while the gas-light came and went
with the breeze of evening.

To be finished on her Sunday off
when she straightened from the pose
and walked around to his side.
And afterwards she drank his tea,
put on her coat and went back to the big house,
her room in the attic.
Or sipped tea
and did not put on her coat.

English Oaks

While the remarkable child plays the latest sonata
Admiral Collingwood excuses himself
and takes the air, out over the lawn,
beyond the Duke's Italian gardens
to the English woods.
It is his custom to stop at intervals,
as if listening to birdsong,
but from the pockets of his breeches
he drops, one by one, the acorns he's brought.

The music now is fitful and barely heard
on the sou' sou' easterly as it rises
to set the trees groaning and panting.
He sees masts of single pine,
the wooden walls of England,
decks of elm, and from each acorn
he presses into grass between the ferns
the keels of the fleet will grow.
There among the buttercups, cowslips,
and the white stars of wild garlic,
England's men'o' war will be seeded
for the sons of his sons.

He treads into rain-softened earth the last one
and slaps his gloves on his leg.
It is a beginning.
The rookery, startled into life, rises
and blackens the sky like a broadside
of shot taken high in the rigging.

Gorse at the Seventh

Tricked again by Christmas,
this mild mid-December spell,
above the green
the south-facing gorse puts out
its strings of yellow flowers.
Tight and sharp, they glint
like candles against the spiky bushes
under the grey end-of-day sky.

A Concorde sounds its booms overhead,
but I know that trick and must look further west
where the silver dart
is already miles along the line,
chasing the sun to New York.
Celebs and the rich popping over to shop
or do the last business of the year –
politics and Donna Karan.

The booms fade away and the traffic
noise is rubbed out by a lift of wind.
A chill end to things with the gorse
flowers cold and waxy
between their angled spikes.
Then a bank of flattened bracken moves
to become a cock pheasant, his eye
above the bright ruff catching mine.

This could be the end of it – a mile
from the clubhouse, the course empty
and the light draining away.
Already street lamps are glowing
into life, the headlights of distant cars,
the airport shaped only by its lit windows.
On the last two holes I'll have to be straight
or lost. No one would know. Not a soul.

Eggs

How your childhood is pieced together.
This Christmas he tells you about
your grandfather
out at night with three caps –
one for his head against the weather,
and one slipped over each boot,
so that he left no print in the snow
across the farmyard to the chickens.
As quiet as snow itself,
under the cracked moon
his hands slipping softly
into the warm, drowsy nests.
And the polished ochre eggs bursting
their bright suns in the morning pan,
one secret and one secret and another.

Glyn

When asked if he believed in God
"Often," he said.
But when I went to see him
the day before he died
there was no sign of light.
Sitting pillowed in bed
he was exhausted by the fight.

We talked of Wales, and friends
and literature,
what we had to write.
I held his left hand
worn as ninety-year-old leather
and tried not to look
at the stump of his other
phantomed in his folded pyjama sleeve.
His eyes were empty and wet.
His hand, light as a feather,
gripped mine like a child's
when I rose to leave.

We were in Boston when we heard he'd died,
but saw the interment of his ashes
two weeks later
in Llansteffan, that small village church
at the mouth of the Towy,
a stone's throw from Fern Hill.
Friends smiled, friends cried.
A Christian gentleman gone before.

Crossing Over

Three days out from England,
The summer-calm Atlantic lulled us with sun
And the last U-boats lay deep like drowsy fish
Waiting for the music of pistons.
Cloudless and hot, so we let the POWs take the air
And a stretch on the after-deck, hundreds of them
In murmuring huddles, bleary and pacing those confines.

Above them, a row of American aircrew headed home,
Perched on the rail facing the bows, away
From the grey dregs of that beaten army.
Those sheepskin and leather flying jackets
We so envied, worn loose now in the heat.
They flexed their arms like boxers lifting weights,
Punching each other in play

And when those strong young men
With their war-tightened faces
Turned to go to the mess, we saw why
They'd broadened their backs above the Germans.
Every man's jacket proclaimed *Berlin Dresden Cologne*
Each raid commemorated with a painted nose-down bomb
Six, eight, eleven missions through the shrapnel.

As we docked at our final berth those fliers
Were soused in bourbon and grew louder,
As men come through it all, against the odds,
Will shout their lives out to the sky,
Slapping backs, jitterbugging man with man,
Then blowing up their last French letters
To launch them as love zepplins towards Manhattan.

Megan's First Snow

Snow came floating through the black night,
your side of the channel, our side,
so here this morning
that dusting on our lawn has settled
in the corners of the garden,
crisp and tightening in the sun.

Not enough left now
to make a shroud or a marriage sheet,
but that patch beneath the privet
could be a gentleman's handkerchief.
Yes, I have decided, for us such token white
shall be *a gentleman's handkerchief*,
our code for what remains of snow,
one of the things only you and I know.

From the Book of Hours

A Nativity, of course,
By the Master of the Circle of Wales,
Provenance – Pembrokeshire, Gwynedd,
And the County of Essex.
Rare: at Sotheby's.

The mother is at the centre,
Her breast its own halo,
That warmth giving the lie to Winter.
The trees are bare, silver and grey
But strong to hold the Spring's growth.

Beyond, through the doorway
A road leads up to the green hill,
The walled edge of a promised city.
The afternoon sky is blue and light
With high clouds touched by gold.

It all comes to this point,
A new beginning.

The border has berries,
Butterflies, song-birds,
And a motif of twining roses,
Red and white.
There are no thorns.

In such a work
An historiated margin might
Well have been anticipated,
While all the prayers and suffrages may be taken
To be on the reverse.

The kings are arriving
Their shoulders hunched, heads bowed,
Offering a superfluity of gifts. Too late -
This daughter's upturned face
Is already alight.

Mapping the World

All maps have ourselves at the centre.
This begins with the Mediterranean,
Then the world the Venetians draw
Moves east to the Turk,
South to the Moor
And the Atlantic route to what will become
The Americas.

All of which was known to Nicolas de Nicolay
Whose *Navigatiom del Mondo Novo*
At the end of the sixteenth century
Pressing up into the colder, darker north
Had Hibernia, Irlande – Scotia and Anglia
As two islands floating at the edge of things.

And Cambria, Cymru, Wales?
Less trouble now than the Irish or the Scots,
Already gone, swallowed by Anglia.
With flat-faced England left to out-stare
A narrow, starving Ireland
And the Virgin Queen a reprobate maiden-warrior
Beyond heaven's reprieve and true prayer.

Floating on the warm, green soup of the lagoon,
No Doge ever craved and ate
The salty lamb of Ceredigion,
A Towy sewin netted and baked.
How could they have dreamt our red kites
Imperiously paired, soaring over Powys?
Our walls of hard, blue slate,
Eryri's streams like chilled Soave
Poured generously over rocks?

And that slow turn on the Ridgeway road
That presents to you the jewelled sea
And holy in the sun
The island of Caldey.

Concerning Some Pictures

I am indebted to your Lordship
for the commission in respect of the works
of M. Canal of his Venice
which I will have despatched this week
with the Venture, bound for Southampton Water,
in trust of your safe receipt.

There being two works –
some three feet six inches in height
by four feet and one inch –
fine views of the Grand Canal and especially
the square of Saint Mark.
Very like the sketches you have already.
Also the width of the lagoon itself is displayed
to effect in the second work.

And if your Grace could agree to the thirty guineas
to be that for the two times twenty sequeens
and the carriage of said paintings to England,
then I remain,

Your humble & obedient servant.

I should add that your Lordship might observe
that M. Canal does not shirk the actual life
of the place and that in the previous work despatched,
to which you expressed something by way of a reserva-
tion,
there is, I recall, a number of barges
of trade and employment arranged
in the right foreground of the Rialto view.
Bargemen and the like busy themselves
and cook beneath their canvas shelters.

The light is an afternoon and shews, I think,
the ancient buildings to best effect.

There is even a woman beating carpets
hung from her balcony; note – another holds a rose.
Beneath, in a corner of her building a man,
it would seem, is passing water – though
this is not to the detriment of the work
and is, I trust, barely discernable.
However, I can well appreciate your Lordship's
sensibilities regarding the latter,
and pray that these new works will not offend.

These two at twenty sequeens will prove of worth,
I vouch. The fellow is whimsical
and varies his prices every day.
And he that has a mind
to have any of his work
must not seem to be too fond of it.

My Lord, the light in this city is almost magical
and this painter – *Canaletto* so characterised –
delivers that truth above all others.
Besides, he is in high reputation here
and people will clamber for his pieces whatever.
Thus, I continue to recommend him,
and remain,

       Sir, your servant.

A Noble Going

We cut his Lordship
from neck to crotch
and taking the guts from the cage
did lay them out and examine the same.

We could appraise from these
that the Lord was in fine fettle for such an age
and that, other things apart, he should have last
to his three score years and ten.

At the table following – Mrs Steer
having laid cold pheasant, well-hung,
that day's bread
and a jug of ruby claret –
there was talk of his leave-taking,
the first peer to be hanged before the crowd.
And he for nought but the shooting of his steward
accused of design and deceit with others
upon his lord and master
over a coal-mine at Ashby de la Zouch.

A noble driven to it in his own landau,
dressed all in his silver-spun, white wedding suit.
And the biggest crowd of the popular
from the Tower to Tyburn,
given three hours of spectacle.
A noble going indeed, despite
the unseeming dispute between executioner
and assistant over five guineas
given by the lord as his fee.

No hanged man ever had the like
of his silk-lined box.
But, I declare, when they lie at last
on our table and we slice –
a lordly gut's
no more jewelled than a slut's.

Dai Greatcoat Visits Waterloo

From the top of the stiff lion's hill
the easterly cuts you to the bone
      on such a man-made moel,
coming from where the maps show Blucher
        and his Huns rushing in to save the day

Wellesley held there
        a fine CO who'd cut his teeth in India
and the Peninsula against the Imperium,
mercenaries, no doubt, on all sides
together with the press'd and conscripted,
      all become Wealcyn.

Seems that Tommy, the good Huns and Orangemen
saw Boney turn heels on that long and blooded day
and slouch back to an island confine
        where, it is said,
the arse-nick'd wallpaper did for him.
A rum story

Cluster'd bleak stone monuments *sans grace* –
Victor Hugo, General Gordon, Hanovarians, Beiges.
It's in the nature of such stuff to make heroes of the brass
while infantry chaps, thousands of 'em,
go into the ground unsung,
      strip't of tunica and boots
and patted down with the flat of a spade.
Memento etiam Domine.
They prized out their teeth for false 'uns.

One feels that neck-tingle
and the pricking of a tear at Hougoumont Farm
where the stout grenadiers – Coldstreams and Jocks,
cursed themselves for hacking down doors
to fire their billy-brew the night before
        that would've been musket rests and firing cover-
but we held the gate against a hard, long day's assault
by Boney's Garde Imperial. They who fell in ranks
within the termini of the farm walls.

Now glimpsed through the grille of the tiny chapel
the feet of our Lord singed that day
are singed for ever.
        Arglwydd – crucified black and grey.

A hundred years peace – until our own Show –
I suppose, was won at that Farm.

        Out on the fields the red line squared up,
bayonets knelt before muskets
        saw their cavalry repulsed
so the poor beasts piled up into bloody parapets.

No need for trenches,
        'cept to bury the fallen –
poor, stripped buggers forever etc.
        some corner of a Belgian field.
Uniforms and personals filched by the infernal followers.

Hand to mouth, hand to hand, the bad breath of the kill.
(Things hardened into the mechanical in our Show
with death dealt out distant, through gun sights)

One moment: old Wellie snapping shut his telescope,
then waving his hat to send our chaps after their rout,
standing high in his stirrups
                    on the bay Copenhagen
to survey the confusion.

Men ploughing the mud
                    with their sweet faces.
In paradisium deducant te Angeli
For there had been no help on that open plain
save the embrace of the enemy.

Turning

Stopping for salt-marsh lamb
from Eynons – *Purveyors of Fine Meats,*

on the Blue Boar bridge in the centre of St. Clears,
if you had not turned to double-check the car

that heron priesting the river
would have remained in the blue-grey shade

of overhanging trees, statuesque, dabbing
into the Cynin's shallow, pebbly flow,

an un-witnessed river-lord,
before turning and loping into the air

Laugharne-wards, spreading
his black, grey and white surplice against the sky.

At Gumfreston Church

That evening, after a hard, hot drive,
The dark lane's coolness of trees
Was like water walked into,
Calm and quiet – no traffic,
Deep shadows,
All the gulls out at sea.

Augustus and Gwen's father
Walked the two miles from Tenby
Every Sunday to play the organ here.
I search for his headstone and find no-one
But Ken Handicott the grocer
I worked for one school summer holiday
Forty years ago.

They leave the church door unlocked:
There is no congregation but the curious passing folk.
And inside is the simple spendour of stone font,
Low wooden roof, draped altar, Norman-built
On earlier significance – St. Teilo, St. Bridget.
The place shivers in the dusk
And moves into another night.

Here were the early missions, saints and sinners
Crossing the Irish Sea, moving east
With their crosses and swords.
Here was a quay, a village the river Ritec
Joined to the sea that led to the world.

And here, behind the church, before the woods
Where the Magdalens brought their lepers,
Still flow the three springs of purity
And healing, coming to us from a depth.
Water that plays the oldest music.

Without thinking
I take a handful
And with wet, cool fingers
Cross myself.

Barafundle Bay

i.m John Tripp

It's late in the day
when I clamber down to the beach,
mid September, the arse end of summer.
Dexter
&
Daisy
SEREN FREUD
written in the sand, letters five feet high.

A stiff Irish wind is playing in my ear
so I turn to the east and look beyond
the bobbing lobster boat,
the red sandstone cliffs of Stackpole,
to Manorbier's castle and white church tower.
Then the western edge of Caldey Island and beyond,
sinking like a black apple into the night,
Dylan's Gower always, John, always
out of reach for us.

The summer's gone over the hill, John,
and I'm no rough weather guest.
The sea curls back into itself.
The surfers and dog walkers have gone:
now I'm the only one.
I choose and pocket three pebbles – limestone
with veins of pink and white.

I take off my socks and shoes to paddle
at the edge of the retreating waves.
Clear, clean and cold, it wraps around my calves.
This feels like dying from the toes up.

John, you might have wished for such a salty end –
our friend Mike coming out of the sea in Normandy
was dead before he hit the sand.
But your heart gave out, bruised and sour,
on your old man's settee in the Whitchurch bungalow,
the early hours tv showing a blizzard of nothing.

The last fishing boat turns away
from its implausibly orange lobster buoy.
One by one I throw my pebbles at the sea.
Barafundle – *the Atlantic lash,* as you said,
will turn *its storm eye on all frivollers* such as we –
Dexter & Daisy and Seren, the sand-scratched names,
John, the living and the dead.

The Plot

Turning off the Ridgeway to the Manorbier road
you linger in second after that slow bend
to take in again the stunning view of Caldey –
beach, lighthouse, monastery – set in the bluest sea,
just before dropping down the corkscrew lane between
high-banked hedges snow-drifted with constellations
of sweet and musty Queen Anne's lace,
the garlic's sour-sweet flowers like distant stars,
and passing over the railway line
to the chapel where your mother
has reserved her plot, the most prudent of things
in this country where the light and the summer sings.

The Final Shift

Called to the foreman's office
at fifteen minutes to five.
You've done your time Stephens,
fifty years. Here's your packet.
Off you go, man, you go early today.
The rope loosed, weight lifted, direction unclear.

He walked to the foundry gates and looked out.
A summer breeze, poppies in the ditch,
elderflower creaming the line of the hedge,
the sky blue, with light, high clouds.
The coal train's whistle coming down the valley,
Then the afternoon hooters.

He pulled his cap on against the sun
and undid his waistcoat buttons one by one.

Slow Worm

After the hottest of April days,
in the late, slanting sun,
there's a bronzed arabesque

lying on the coping stone
of your herb-border wall – the bright
gold torc of a Silerian queen

pulled up into the light –
that's slid back between the cool bricks,
just now as I looked away

And because you are not here
I must fashion these words
into a shape you'd wear.

Eight Pegs

1.

Thirty notes pressed into a handshake:
Will you take a bird, Sir?
Declined.
        Though you have to step aside
or over this pallet of peacock-bright pheasants,
soft-grey and orange-bronze partridge,
as you leave the Hall and take to your car.
A pallet of abundance, Van Aelst or
Bueckelaer, the way the Dutch laid out
the spoils of the hunt: game,
God's bounty, the good taste of life.

2.

This Emilio Rizzini 12-bore over-under
becomes familiar as the day goes on.

The way when broken
it rests in the crook of your arm.

3.

Eight pegs along the south side of the copse:
the beaters work left to right, flag-waving,
dog-whistling, slapping against the trunks.
The Keeper shouts "rise" or "now" –
something I can't understand – until
to my right the double cracks begin to thud and echo
and a pheasant – "a good bird" –
clatters down a ladder of branches.

4.

The looker from Llandeilo crosses the stream
with a partridge on each breast, hanging
from the game hooks on her tunic.
Breast on breast, they roll and bounce
with life as she comes our way.

5.

The Well-stocked Kitchen: duck, hare,
grouse, grapes, partridge, artichoke,
rabbit, nuts, marrow, a leg of the lamb: Christ
in the house of Martha and Mary.

6.

This one has hunted Big Game
in seven African countries.
He is dapper: checked jacket, waistcoat and plus twos.
A green tie knotted neatly into his checked collar.
Last week, Idaho, the Black Bear.

My son (the Paras, SAS) runs a gun school there:
S.W.O.T. teams, special forces,
furious business since the Towers and the Muslims.
Got a rib pushed through one lung
dropping from a Hercules low over the jungle:
dealing with Bolivian drugs. In/out
finish them off. Couple of hundred feet.
Hairy business. But what he's trained to do.

The Black Bear's found all over,
but they can be brown or grey or cinammon.
Roosevelt, the first one, Theodore,
took a lot of them. Taste's like good pork.

7.

Beginner's luck: the first on the third drive
coming low out of the trees of the slope
above the noisy stream. Right to left,
then juddering to a halt in mid air,
falling in on itself to land, absurdly soft,
at the feet of the fourth peg.

The second on the fifth drive, out
of a high copse from one-o-clock
in full flight from what it heard
into what it couldn't have imagined.
The promise of a blue sky escape,
then a prat-fall through air to carry
over the road and crumple in the next field.

8.

Clutched in my left hand for the photograph –
how weighted in death, how soft
the neck between fingers and thumb;
the dull eyes in its flopping head,
its rainbow crop, its flecked and striped wings
the pointillist flicker of bracken and woods:
all the colours of the world, still moving.

from Gelligaer Common

Make us, O Lord, a people fit for poetry – Idris Davies

7.

Walk off the Wall
into a sky cut clear and immense
over Cwm Bargoed and the Common.

Above the coal train, above
the kestrel hung over the cwm,
the weather wind lifts and carries you

over the platform houses' medieval palimpset,
over grey fistfuls of sheep,
a skitter of ponies,

the abstracts of heather and dumped rubbish,
over the growling boy-racer who slows
and slows and comes down to a crawl

to stop beside that Cwm Rhymney view
and then, yes, because the moment also chooses him,
looks back and up at you.

The poems from Gelligaer Common were first published in the booklet "Common Sense"; the project was undertaken with poet Grahame Davies, painter Gigi Jones and composer Mervyn Burtch. Booklet and accompanying DVD of the music and other footage appeared in 2013.

8.

On Mynydd Fochriw
we stand above the ruins of Dowlais
as the slopes are levelled for coal
and the tipped black shale glints back at you.

The long slow trains
clatter from here to the sea,
from the place of derelict furnaces
to the Aberthaw promontory.

So, Idris bach, who's to say
when they've scraped the last of the crop
and those wide scars of flattened hills
are grassed into neat table tops

and kids kick balls and shout
and run with their shirt-tails flapping out
and the ledgers are loaded with profit and loss,
who's to say the wind and rain will give a toss?

10.

Kevin's pony wouldn't be led that day
across our playground at the Welfare.
He became skittish, spooked
and sensed that under his hoofs was little but air,
the old workings of the George pit.
So that was how they were traced and gated,
made safe at the foot of the hill where we played.

Under the grass, under our games,
the coal roads led nowhere, were worked out
and the voices of miners,
all those songs and jokes and banter
and pride and deep hurt
did no more than whisper to ponies.
Listen, they said, *these are our names.*

from The Alchemy of Water

This is the alchemy of water:
from the floating forms of low cloud, mist,
are beaten these pendants of silver

*

The Falls stitch ribbons, lace
into (sometimes) sheets,
(sometimes) shrouds.

*

Cloud splinters forth over Bala –
God's grandeur of lent light –
Gerard Manley Hopkins,
Cecil B. de Mille.

*

In the land of slate-blue, slate-black,
slate-brown, slate-green,
these hands of low cloud
bearing a platter of light.

*

One of those houses you'd imagine
living in: a blanket of trees, a scarf of mist,
your neighbours the mountains.
And each morning a garden of water.

*

The suck and pull of shingle
by a tide subtle and lacy.
On the horizon a whale and her calf:
you wait for them to move.

*

Pentre Ifan's pall bearers
process with the sharp slab held high.
In the stones' shadows
dew settles like tears.

*

Dawn over Swansea Bay:
Dylan's ugly, lovely town.
The wet sand is filling with sky.
The boat's chains are a rich and heavy necklace.

Those rust-ochre links will tie you to this place
Whatever the rise of the tide,
Whatever the blue-grey weather brings,
Whenever the sea sings in these chains.

*

The green-aged stone wall
and rusting wire: what are they keeping out,
or in? The thorn tree in Winter
hangs its Christmas lights of rain.

*

The Irish Sea plays its old game –
breathing in, breathing out,
sending its salt-shining
tribute to the field's precipitous plunge.

*

Unless you master the natural jigsaw of stone,
placing the stone kisses, cheek to cheek,
you cannot square the wet hills into sheep pastures,
angle against the stream's riots, the mist's confusions

*

Bridges defy water,
are defined by water.

Streams and waterfalls are the emissaries
of sky and mountain.

In the politics of rivers
negotiations are ongoing.

*

Here the dead are fenced above the shore.
They have ridden out the storm.

The ebb and flow of the green-grey sea
needs an age to weather their names,
an age to tilt a memory.

From the Fortunate Isles

On the concrete walkway by the Playa de la Calera
he has arranged his beads and locusts
on a curl of palm bark,
the whole set off by a sprig of bougainvillea
snapped from the municipal's border.

The thinness of this beach flaneur
is deliberate: spindly mahogany arms and legs,
tight beard and haphazard rasta dreads.

Our paella is brought in a sizzling metal pan,
then arranged by the waiter in and around
the lipped glass bowls as if the pattern signified.

As I pull apart the last of my prawns
the beach bum, the mahogany maker
has completed another leaf, pin and twig locust.
He places it on his palm curl display
and wanders back down to the black sand beach
where every seventh Atlantic roller
pulled by the turning planet
pounds here on its way to Africa,
raising then spilling a clutch of surfers.

He stops for no reason and then, for no reason, returns
past the clumsy drop-out juggler
with his battered club and the ragged baton twirler
caught somewhere between the Shankill and New Orleans.

No-one buys, no-one surely will ever
buy the locusts or the beads.
His older self, forty years on, wrinkled and bronzed
slouches by and clicks down each of the pay-phone levers:
no change, no cigar, no cherry –
the way, I remember, Ratso did in Midnight Cowboy,
collar up and hunched in freezing Manhattan.

And why not in such a place under this sun,
with the thundering, deep green, sparkling sea,
the pendulous purple flower and fruit of each banana tree,
let loose of it all and be a beach bum?
I fiddle with the lens of my Nikon.

Two at Manorbier

You are that seal's head bobbing between crests
as you lie on the waltzing board
feeling each swell, taking the sea's pulse
waiting for the next wave,
just one more, your last of the day,
to sweep you back to a point between
the castle and the white bell tower
to the sloping sand and smoothed pebbles

where she sits waiting:
and when you call through the waves' crash,
when you raise your arms,
she shields her eyes against the dropping sun
to pick you out, and smiles;
though you can't see, you know she smiles.

From Brunel Quay

I look over to Hobb's slipway
where my father would drive us on to the chugging ferry
for its short drift here across the Cleddau;
years before that concrete bridge framed the sky
and river to link the county.
One of the anglers has pulled out a green-grey wrasse
glinting from the brown waters of the Haven.

This stretch of estuary mud and water
is where my Uncle Ivor took us on his new boat
up the disappearing curves of the Cleddau
– Mill Bay, Beggars Reach, Llangwm Pool –
all the way to Haverfordwest quay
one calm and sunny day in 'fifty-eight;
that was after the refinery had paid him a fortune
for the Old Rectory and his fields of earlies
and just before his heart gave out.

On Brunel Quay where the Great Western
would connect us to the world
the engineer's plinth has been stripped of its statue,
– that tough little man with stove-pipe hat and a fistful of plans –
sawn-off in the early hours and scrapped for bronze cash;
but now the evening comes alive with the wriggling fish
this angler weighs and measures
then lifts to his lips like a lover.

He bites through the line an inch from its open mouth
and drops the old lady, y gwrach, the wrasse
back into the gentle slap of the tide.
These new hooks dissolve, he says.
It all dissolves.

Wyeth's *Liberty Launch*

Beached in the meadow
before the house in its winter darkness.
The cold light turns the salt-worked planks
white. This is the ghost of a boat:
the half-remembered fishing trips,
passage between the islands,
its mooring rope sunk in the grasses.

The keel's peeling paint is red
going to brown, the propeller's missing
and the shaft is rust-tight.
Out of water, the rudder is a quarter moon
pointing dead ahead.
Beyond the house, the coast of Maine,
you know the ocean quickens its dance.

Clay

i.m. Morgen Hall

This is the way she works:
she takes a sliced image of the things it can hold –
broccoli, tagliatelle, celery, spaghetti –
and presses their computed ghosts into the clay
she fires into permanent forms.
See her vessels and plates with ridged dimples
and the thumb-prints of her cross-sectioned celery,
the flowery curls of her saucers and cups,
the arabesques of patterned spoons
that play in your fingers.

This is the way it works:
they have taken a paper-thin slice
of her breast
and pressed the ghost of her cancer to the lens
for the computer to read. See
the wild shapes of it, the cathedral's smashed stained-glass,
Shylock's fistful of flesh cast into the flames.
Then the firing, the thrown chemicals,
the burning through to a shape that will last,
the closest thing to permanence a potter can make.

Coram's Cloths

This hole cut in my dress that I worry and enlarge
with fingering is where the piece was taken
by them at the Foundlings as token
when I left my precious in their charge.

Whereby that cloth shall be the means,
they say, for me to recognise myself to her
when the world's workings and men's schemes
shall turn to mine and her favour.

Though the nights grow frost
and my fortunes tip. By then, I fear, the space
of my worrying will surely not fit
to the piece they kept, and wrote beside *Alice*.

Seeking Gwen John

The station at Meudon de Fleury,
Still as she would have known it –
Arts and Crafts brickwork – a promise
Of the careful tidiness of the town.
And then that slow climb up the hill to her place.

But today the view of Paris from the Terrasse
Is foreshortened – pollution.
Five straight days of a smoky haze
And the mayor has declared the Metro and the RER free.
From rue Terre Neuve, her top-floor appartement,

She would have seen the Tour Eiffel,
In this sharp Spring air, even Montmartre.
Today the view is dabbed flat
With a dry brush of pigmented air
In the manner of her meticulous art.

The house has gone:
There's a modernist, expensive cube
With, at an upstairs window,
An easel.
Neighbours at the rear know nothing of Gwen.

L'Eglise Saint Martin is lighter than her back pew
Surreptitious sketches show:
A view of the nuns and their orphans.
These stained-glass windows would have been new,
Fresh light opening up the place.

She is not here. There is no trace.
The woman in the Accueil knows nothing of her;
A plaque mentions only Rabelais,
Their local cure centuries back.
The African priest shrugs, smiles, then a blank face.

Nor is she at Rodin's house, the Meudon Musée now,
Except a plaster version of her as the Whistler Muse.
It is cold, deathly pale and we pose beside it for a photo.
The curator knows nothing of her:
'After Camille Claudel,' she says, 'he had many lovers.'

Gwen would have surely been pleased:
Shunning unlooked-for company till the end.
Sufficient – her sketchbook, her cats, her God.
On the rue Terre Neuve in this thin sun there is no ghost:
The bank of municipal daffodils are a swaying host.

Our Little Horovitz

Put to the piano at six
It was Miss Morgan's at Rowan View
Every Thursday after school.
A stuffed fox in the hall
And a Garrad Westminster chime on the mantle
That confused the metronome.

You were paid for by Auntie Gwyneth
Who like Florence Morgan,
Never call her Flossie, mind,
Had letters after her name.

Six streets away and further up the valley's side
Houses had names and fronts
With lawns and hydrangeas
And windows big enough to need nets.
There were hedges, a monkey puzzle tree,
And the doctor's Alvis at Willow Bank.

You sat tight on Flossie's stool and never dared ask
For the convenience indoors.
The ladder of scales was climbed and climbed again
Until you were dizzy and numb,
Up to the summit – Grade Four:
Though Beethoven can do without the Boogie-Woogie
She declared when rhythm got the better of you.
But still your fingers itched and your toes danced
In those pinching, polished best shoes
Until the lesson's end.
In the hall the fox glass-eyed your goodbye.

You tumbled back down the hill like a runaway dram of coal,
The one that had taken two fingers
From your father's right hand
Down the Lady Margaret the year before.

The Seventy-First

Things did not start well:
we were tossed violently in St George's Channel
a week and more off the coasts of Ireland and Wales
and though it were June the seas ran in mountains
so that we must make for Portsmouth from the gales.

In that harbour when some two dozen of our men
to take the air from the stifled press below-decks
stood and held to the lashings at the side,
a swell rose and pitched them into the sea.

We came about as best we could and threw
all manner of things to them – barrels, even hen coops.
But failing, ten or so went down and then
John McComie diving to their aid
in casting off his trews got tangled
and sank with the rest.

Days later we made Ostend, then Ghent and Brussels,
and our engagement with the French at Waterloo
was no more than a week after that.

There we prevailed, though lost many:
their artillery got our range and cut an avenue
from the first company to the tenth
with one shot that took apart sixty men.

The local people had a fine harvest from that field:
clothes and muskets, possessions and teeth.

On our route to Paris everything we came across
laid waste by our Prussian friends; except
one farm where Moorhead,
who had a good countryman's nose,
discovered a fowl house undetected.
He made play with his sabre and that night we feasted,
Long and Moorhead and I, victorious Lieutenants three
before a warming hearth and bed.

And as I slept I saw again what had brought us to this –
the broken bones, horses and men.
I felt the furnace sun, tasted the brackish
murderous water at the Cape;
smelt the beautiful horses we'd shot
on the beach at St Lucia to save
them from the French.

Then those screams
as John McComie's hand reached to us
from the waves. Such dreams.

Shillings and pence

South of Mametz on the Fricourt road
shrapnel felled his frantic horse
and the toppled gun carriage snapped his arm
then ground him in the mud.

Hours later they found him,
taken for a corpse, 'til one eye
blinked open to the lightening sky.

Weeks with the white nuns; then
the long journey back to Ystrad Mynach,
with his working arm stuck out absurdly
in splints above his bandaged head: this Blighty
gift taken before his seventeenth birthday.

Three long days from Albert to home:
the khaki-crammed platforms,
songs and moans and steam and waiting,
a succession of dusty carriages and platitudes.

When in his mother's parlour she helped him out
of that coarse uniform, it weighed a ton:
tunic, trouser pockets, kit-bag filled with coins –
the King's shillings, the people's pennies
slipped quietly to the boy while he'd stood or slept
by the men and women he'd travelled with.

That evening before the hearth, her fire coaxing
the numbing cold from out of him,
he saw the flickering future and slept the night
awkwardly, there in his father's chair.

The Blue Grave Of Corfu

Each morning in the half-light
the young Serbian boys slip over the side of the boat
into the water.
                It is Winter –
the straits are inky dark and cold.

They turn over and press their bony heads
into the five fathoms.
                   They have been rowed
far enough from Vidos Island
so that the waters can bed them.
There's little left but their bones and,
skeletal, they dive out of history.

This is after the long march, tactically away
from the Austrians, past the sniping Albanians,
through the callous snows of the mountains.
They have left behind the old and the pregnant women:
in national dress some are hanged from crucifixes.

The army has stumbled on, leaving the fallen, the weak.
They have danced with dysentery,
                      have laid down
with tuberculosis, typhus. Now they shrink back
into the loneliness of themselves, huddled
in the make-shift tents of British sails and oars.
From the gnarled olive and rocky island
the boat ferries back and forth to their common blue grave
and Charon's the Greek.

In the summer months of that year
the azure waters grow warm
                       and for five more summers
after the war, the Corfiots will cast no nets there,
take no fish fed from the blue grave of the Serbs.

The sands will marrow their limbs
to an ivory white.
                  They compose a brief coral reef;
there are lobsters and silver bass that were their flesh.

Patton's Lippizans

That was the strangest damn thing I saw,
an afternoon in April when General Patton
took charge of the horses they'd brought up from Vienna,
saving them from being meat for the Russians,
the day before the day they called a halt to the war.

So that marked the end of our journey –
from Omaha Beach, the Normandy hedges,
the Ardennes's final German push, the massacre at Malmedy.
And that place in the woods, Buchenwald,
with the walking skeletons and the stench of death.

Now the Kraut Podhajsky puts on a fine show
with the Lipizzans in formation –
legs like the *corps de ballet*, high-stepping in slow motion,
then rearing up in the air as if held by strings –
for he had been a cavalry officer in the First War.

And four-star crazy General George returns his hats-off salute
with one of his own: horseman to horseman.
Unsaddled and loosed, those white stallions ran into the pastures –
they were magnificent in the afternoon sun,
perfect like a peace-time picture-card.

These were special, reared in stud, not the poor beasts
that had charged the Panzers in Poland and were minced.
Nor pack animals pulling guns or refugees
under the Stukas on the roads in Belgium and France
or in the Krauts' retreat from Stalingrad.

Born and reared in the high mountains
from classy stock over centuries; they turn
after their fourth year from black and blue and bay
to shades of white and grey.
As we in four years of war have grown as pale as bone.

Following the Horses

At fifteen, too young to plough, he was put to harrow
With two of his father's shire horses,
Old enough and wise enough to know their own way.

Sometimes in the length of that summer
He'd even hitch a ride on the roller –
Bird song, dreaming, not a care.

That year his clenched fists on handle and reins
Chafed and blistered and calloused
Into the roughness of a man's.

Jasper and Ned made steady progress through the long afternoon
To tea-time. Then over his shoulder
An approaching thunder, rumbling low and then louder

With the roar of a Wellington dragging its shadow
Over the fields that spooked both horses and boy, so he'd run
Forward to their huge, startled heads and talked them down.

The bomber skimmed over Painters Coppice, limping
Towards Hampstead Norreys, from its port engine
A pall of smoke across the trees and into the evening sky.

That night in the White Hart his father heard them say
The landing had been a close thing,
The pilot tough and skilled at twenty-three.

But Tail-End Charlie, barely older than the plough-boy,
Had caught it – his shrapnelled guts held in by
The navigator's arms until the ambulance came.

Seventy years on he wonders what the ending might have been:
Air crews didn't speak of what they'd seen
Except through nods and looks and silences.

That day: the smell of turned earth, clear blue skies
Etched with dark smoke, the reek of burning oil
Silencing the birds. And the horses' wide eyes.

Gettysburg

In the Seminary Ridge Museum
the ward rooms have figures of the wounded –
a shattered leg, a bloody bandaged head;
one young man propped in bed
with the Good Book in his hands.
Seven of them, life-like: imagine the low moans
shocked wide eyes, blood etching the floorboards.
From other rooms the screams, saws working through bones.
Through the windows more traffic, waggons,
horses clatter across the gravel.

*

On the third day: one last Confederate fling –
Pickett's Charge across the meadows to Cemetery Ridge
was heroic and desperate.
Now those North Carolina men are larger-than-life bronzes;
they surge forward from their plinth as one,
tumbling into a shared grave.
And this was the high water mark of the Confederacy:
Lee's army withdrew at midnight, back down
the long road through the Appalachian foothills,
back to the South, and two more long years of defeat.

*

In the Fall's yellow and orange woods
the Old War Horse Longstreet still rides,
forever turning his shoulder to check
his troops along the Seminary Ridge.
Luxuriantly bearded, he is resolute,
reins and stirrups taut and braced,
his wisdom dismissed by Robert E. Lee.
He sees behind him Pickett's doomed charge,
a noble, foolhardy failing to buck the odds.
At the horse's rear hoof someone has planted a tiny Dixie flag .

*

From Little Round Top, General Warren
and his Army of the Potomac held fast the heights
and from here with sharpshooters and ordnance
pinned down the charging rebels.
Days after the battle Matthew Brady's men
broke the legs and arm of a dead Confederate boy
to pose him for that sniper's shot below in the Devil's Den.
In those Gettysburg photographs all's held statue-still.
Whatever charges, explodes, cuts and parries
could only blur and fade, drift past.
Faces and uniforms of the living and the dead
were fragile, monochrome ghosts printed on glass.

*

Sheltered at the rear of the Pennsylvania memorial
this weekend the companies of re-enactors are bivouaced –
Vermont, New Hampshire, Maine,
their cars parked discreetly out of sight.
Ordered lines of flimsy canvas and period blankets
they've slept under through two nights of chilly late September.
I see no wristwatch, the Union blues are authentic –
un-pressed, rough against my neck and wrists
when they insist I try them on, grip the Enfield carbine.
The photo of me, cropped at the waist,
does not show my deck shoes, shorts, as I shoulder arms.

*

On Sunday we walk the Union's right flank,
where the Fishbone of their positions began to curl;
crossing the brook below Culp's Hill,
along Slocum Avenue winding through the quiet wood,
memorial plaques and stones stationed on both sides of the disputed road.
Summer's at an end. Migrating starlings gather
to unfurl their black flag in the sky.

Pro Patria

Cowardice:
too sharp a word for that dull
ache in your guts turning to water
at the thought of crossing the sea –
Biscay, the Med., Sicily, the war pushing up
through the boot of Italy and now,
at last, surely, bound for Germany:
the embarkation camp at Hucknall.

So when the corporal barked that order
you refused,
would not bear arms, load your rifle,
slide a bullet into the breech.
All that had been hammered in to you,
the basics they'd drilled through the middle of you,
everything they'd tried to teach,
after four and a half years finally grown brittle;
tired of the fusty stale rub of the coarse uniform,
the bull-shit polished 'til it gleamed.

There on parade in front of all the men,
Eager, reluctant, or bored,
some open-mouthed at what you'd done,
but keeping mum.
So that the C.S.M. was sent for,
then the Colonel, then the court convened.

Did you mutter, remain silent, head down?
Or offer a statement of principle, the pacifist line?
There's nothing in your service record
and nothing kept in the Archives at Kew.
Were you mute, coherent, blubbering? Or firm,
with your arguments practised?
Which of those persons did we think we knew?

Whatever happened, the whole thing's been
washed away – personal feelings, the loss of face,
a Field General Court Martial
before they packed you off to Lincoln Prison
and a cell alongside the ne'er do wells,
Quakers and spivs, malingerers, wastes of space.

Then released, coming home
and concealing that disgrace: "A half-track
went over my foot." My arse.
How did you keep a straight face?
Sent back to be of use servicing Land Army trucks
and hiding the fact, whatever it was, from us
for the rest of your life, thirty-four years.

All those war films we watched, Dad,
In Which We Serve, The Dam Busters, Reach for the Sky:
"I always wished that I'd joined the RAF," you'd say.
The Airfix kits we glued and painted –
Lancaster, Spitfire, Messerschmitts
to dog-fight from my bedroom ceiling.

But best of all the Sunderland Flying Boat's perfect white;
now those armed swans I know you watched
for the first two years of the war,
rising from and splashing back into Milford Haven,
patrolling the Irish Sea.
That's in your record, of that we can be sure,
ack-ack guns, searchlights, just as you told me.

The rest's left to my imaginings, what you botched,
bent, funked, fudged, all that shite.
Pages of bare facts, regiments, postings, dates,
in those desk wallahs' practised copperplate;
there is no more.

In Budapest

This month's newly-minted moon
a communion wafer
held in the mouth of Andrassy Street:
it shines like a pilgrim's token,
like a circle of guilt.

The only synagogue with a burial ground
within its walls, Dohany Street: these two thousand dead
the Red Army found, starved, frozen
in piles on the streets of the shrunken ghetto.
The ones that missed the trains.

★

The bronze shoes memorial on the Pest bank of the Danube
glows in the autumn sun:
this is where the Arrow Cross fascists
marched families to the river and shot them.
The bodies swept downstream, turning blue.

★

These are the names of the Righteous Among the Nations:
Raoul Wallenberg, Katalin Karady, Sara Salkahazi,
Margit Slachta, Carl Lutz, Vilmos Apor, Kalman Ferenczvalvi;
those who pleaded the human cause, who shuffled the papers,
juggled the accounts, printed the passports – sorcerers of survival.

★

Our bodies pressed shoulder to cheek in the steam chamber;
we try to make out the others' faces: The Szechenyi Baths.
We are in the cooking heat together: lavender,
heather, aromas you can't quite place.
Back outside under the cold, blue sky we walk
into the green pool, the sulphurous water up to our necks.

★

It is the festival of Sukkot: the Hasidic man, long, black overcoat,
neat black beard, hands to a child in the queue for the synagogue tour
a lulav of bound palm, willow and myrtle, ear of corn,
in his other hand a firm, green etrog fruit:
celebrate what God gives, what we give to others.

This month's newly-minted moon
held in the mouth of Dob Street
like a communion wafer:
it shines like a pilgrim's token,
a reminder of our shame.

A History of the World in 101 Objects

And this, from the later Twentieth Century,
nineteen forty-seven, to be precise,
though much in evidence to the present day.

There is a rightness about the implement,
fitting as it does the grip of both young and old,
serviceable under all conditions of politics and duress
and in all climates, extremes of hot and cold.

The quality of manufacture ensures
a uniform and reliable performance.
Simplicity of function means it is
easily maintained in field conditions,

and, allowing for the weight, even
a child or malnourished adult may carry
and use the piece to great effect,
girl or boy, woman or man.

The arc of fire is generous,
though accuracy it may be noted
must be sacrificed to the efficacy of the scythe.

This is the Ram's Horn, the Cuerno de Chivo –
it has decorated the flags of causes and nations
from Moscow to Mozambique to Mexico.
It has been converted into a guitar.

It is said that the inventor of the piece
had ambitions to be a poet:
instead, wounded in the defence
of his homeland, he designed this.

And for over sixty years who is to say
more or fewer poems have come from its use:
the chattering metre, the rhyme,
the stanzas and epics of the AK?

For Queen and Country

Six weeks of basic training on the Wiltshire Downs
living cheek by jowl beyond the reach of family and towns

forty boys in each Nissen hut becoming men
for Queen and Country; Nasser, Suez. And then

one long evening after a full-kit march,
sore and blistered and stiff as starch,

after horsing about in the scalding showers
two new-found mates got slapping towels

'til arms and legs and private parts
were chaffed and stung. *Fucks* and farts

petered out and then around the watching ring
the claps and taunts two fighters bring

from any crowd dropped down and died
as, fascinated, those clutching togas tried

to jostle for a better view of the two prickateers
who, erect and starkers

hip-swung their stiffened rogers like swords
until they spurted each in turn. Barely a word

then, as some had slunk away in shame
and others open-mouthed tried to find the name

for what they had been spectators to.
Each lodged in his narrow bunk. The two

gladiators, beds apart, with final boasts – *Champion!*
Thee thinks tha's cock of the walk, son?

And after Lights Out those mucky, murky dreams of legs and breasts –
Marilyn Monroe, Diana Dors. Then desert flies. Then death.

Andrew Wyeth's *Snow Hill*

In December snow we've raised a Maypole of pine:
Atop a wagon wheel and baby spruce,
With ribbons from each spoke for the dance.
These are the living and the dead, the dearest friends of mine.

For all my people at the last
Shall dance up on Snow Hill.
Under the Christmas tree and wheel
They join hands, circling still.

Each has a place, each has a ribbon:
In his Kaiser's War helmet and greatcoat,
Boots parade-polished after the Marne,
Karl Keurner holds the hand of Anna,
His grey and tiny wife.
Here they dance together,
Step more lively than ever in life.

All my people at the last
Are dancing on Snow Hill.
Under the Christmas tree and wheel
They join hands, circling still.

Anna holds Bill Loper's good hand,
His other, the right, was lost on the railroad
Years back, but father never let me paint it.
"We don't need that," he said,
Taking his cloth to wipe it clean away.
But I painted *Little Africa* with socket,
Strap and hook when both of them were dead.

All my people at the last
Are dancing on Snow Hill.
Under the Christmas tree and wheel
They join hands, circling still.

Bill's hooked to Helga, her coat
A rich, dark green, her blonde hair in plaits
Flying as the ribboned circle turns when she steps out
And drives the whole dance.
She sets the clock backwards and pulls to the right.
Queen of the woods, my secret muse,
Could turn the seasons with a glance.

All my people at the last
Are dancing on Snow Hill.
Under the Christmas tree and wheel
They join hands, circling still.

Helga's holding Allan Lynch
Whose mind went long before he passed.
I painted him as me, my spirit
Running downhill the day my father died.
I wore his hunter's flap-eared hat
Against the cold cutting through my heart.
These are my folk, close and kindred.

All my people at the last
Shall dance up on Snow Hill.
Under the Christmas tree and wheel
They join hands, circle still.

The sixth ribbon is mine.
I hold it firm as a brush loaded with cobalt blue:
A blue this sky has blotted out,
The blue of shadows under hedges
In deep winter. Such a blue as Tom lay in
On his day bed in the garret room
For his last days back in sixty-two.

The seventh ribbon's white,
It blows around untended
And waits for Christina. Her arm's stretched out,
This dance has not yet ended.

Holsteins Black and White.

Now we are down to our last ten Holsteins
when my father had kept a hundred.
And still the bombers sweep overhead
– Bremen, Hamburg, Berlin, –
is there anything left to bomb in Hamburg?
So it is over. And we all know that it is over.
But still we are to deal with the prisoners.

My grandfather's saying, "A happy beast makes happy meat."
And we have followed that.
Though it is so long since we tasted beef.
We keep our beasts happy and ordered: play loud music
to cover the shots – marches, Wagner if Hans is feeling classy,
even Der Lambeth Valk – that Jewish mischief
which Hans has kept despite the ban.

Name. Number.
Now come into this room;
we shall weigh you, and our doctors will check your health
before we put you to work.
And your teeth,
especially important is the teeth.
Now stand against that wall for the height measurement…

And that is when we slid open the panel
and put a bullet into the back of his neck.
Hans and I take turns with the rifle and the panel.
A hundred, a thousand shots and so on until
there is no point in counting. No faces: just their napes.
We have bags of teeth fillings; though few from the Russians.
And for this work I have home leave.

There are no doctors at this point.
Herr Doctor Heinz Baumkotter would not waste
time on this work. The SS men
simply put on white coats and see the charade through.
The Herr Doctor has his experiments
which, from what I hear, makes humane
what Hans and I and the others do.

I have four more days on the farm.
My mother copes as best she may on her own
though the sky turns red most nights. If I could have stayed...
The Holsteins are all in the bottom field
and huddle together as if they know something
of the world. I could work a life and breed from those ten.

Sachsenhausen

From The Needles

After the barber's pole lighthouse on chalk stilts,
There's Julia Margaret Cameron's wet plate studies – Tennyson,
Dickens, Alice, and Herschel's wild sky glare – portraits
Still breathing one hundred and fifty years on.

Then we drive from Freshwater Bay to Compton Beach
Where the brochure's shown a family fossil hunting.
The cliffs drop sheer, white and ochre and peach,
With earth, flint and chalk slithering.

But the Fossil Forest gives us nothing:
Just two flint shapes my foot turns over.
Interestingly pierced pieces –
One a smoothed cylinder with crystallised hollow core.

Holding this up to the sky frames a flower of blue.
This shall be *a caveman's telescope* for Megan and Ellis
And I'll instruct them in its use.
Midway to the horizon I fix on a trawler:

Grey and cream and rust, it fills the flower aperture,
Simply gives one instance of the world,
The way a found fossil, a still-life, an Alfred Wallis ship
Strikes you – a poem, a single note, an open shutter.

Oh you! Who have your eye-balls vexed and tired,
Feast them upon the wideness of the sea: true,
and by this caveman's telescope inspired
Keats might have proved less is more, as poets do.

Poems from the National Trust Residency at Dyffryn Gardens in the Vale of Glamorgan

Waggons

They owned more waggons than anyone else
so that day after day
coal trains longer than imagining
were pulled by ropes of steam
on purposeful lines from pits to docks and back again –
Cory. Cory. Cory. Cory. Cory....
past pit villages, under bridges;
so many that mischievous boys
chucking clods for play
would lose count, grow bored and turn for home.

And when Reginald planted and bred
more dahlias than anyone else in Wales,
the garden boys and hands lost count.
He'd hunted down stars and pompons,
whose duty it is to swagger and flaunt,
hold high their blousy heads.
A long winter and spring waiting
for those tubers to bring forth blooms
and colours exotic without number, beyond imagining.
Mariner, Little Othello, Mafeking.

Distance travelled

Jets keep tally in chalk-marks across the sky
over Dyffryn's measured gardens,
plying to those places where the Corys'
business stretched across the oceans,
driven by steam, powered by Welsh anthracite.

And now at Tenerife in Los Christianos Bay
where coal loaders sweated to re-fuel, day and night,
freighters, frigates, His Majesty's ships of the line,
the grandchildren of miners are at play,
for even the Valleys people are well-travelled.

The Empire that we built has long gone,
colonies and trading ports are leisure destinations.
The world the owners ruled has unravelled,
and no-one now, praise be, knows his proper station.

The Circle of Oaks

Some Sundays, when I am able,
I make my excuses – a chill, cramps,
what her Ladyship calls "vapours",
and go not to worship but to this tree circle,
which is all the church I need,
for Williams the footman reckons
that is where they buried her.

A day old at most, she was.
I was taken with high fever
and can remember little of it
but her gripping my finger,
then cook's cold flannels and warm broth;
the slow recovery and the healing,
she says that will some day be complete.

Un-christened, except for the water
I bring most times in a kitchen cup
to sprinkle these tree roots each in turn,
for I know not under which she was lain.
They say there have been other serving girl's mistakes,
so I bless them all with my sprinkling
and my kneeling prayers.

From our quarters under the roof
I watch the stars rise over these woods, listen
to the owls, a hawk taking a leveret;
fur and bones on the morning lawn.
I skirt the rose borders they have planted,
all the flowers that may offer girls a name.
And beneath each tree, clock fashion, I say them.

Quartet for Two Painters

Peter Prendergast and Iwan Gwyn Parry

Prendergast's Quarry

Bruised skies tumble over Eryri
drenching the land
under the god-governed, paper-torn clouds
until the colours run

through that squat stone chapel,
and the church spire's spike,
where the houses huddle
between stone walls at Deiniolen.

Rain slips blue light down slate slopes
and settles in the black cauldron of Penrhyn.
Weather and the water's clock
happens whether you paint it or not.

Today, the wind cuts in from Ireland
to the avalanche of slate held at Bethesda,
splinters of the quarry's bone, flakes of slate skin,
settled under its own weight.

In your last wicker bed
you lie, Peter, and one by one
we sprinkle our fingers of earth on you.
You chose this landscape and it takes you in.

Reaching Yr Achub

This is what you would have wished:
when they heard, the quarry men offered a gift,
took your sons up with them
to the face above the town
to choose a slab from the rare, green vein.

Dressed, polished and inscribed: *Painter and teacher*
it will weather through the hard winters
in this corner of Bethesda's cemetery. Rest easy,
Peter, on your right shoulder the Penrhyn quarry,
at your left Ynys Mon and then the Irish sea.

The Visit

Forgetting flowers, this time
I take a Manorbier pebble
from the car

and, in the ancient way,
lay it on your grave:
my seal-grey limestone on your green slate.

Smooth, fitting my grip,
it feels like the memory of a hand shake
or a hand on shoulder or hip;
the natural form
of a chosen tool –
a hammer, a pencil, a brush.

Meeting Point

This was where his heart stopped
on a path through the slate country

walking to Llanberis.
Just here, Peter died, they said.

And then, just then, on a low branch
you recognised a redstart –

a flash of pure white on his head,
his flickering chest and tail a strong red.

You heard that song,
a clear summer flute:

rare migrant, brief visitant.
And from that time,

Iwan, you tell me
you take it for a sign.

Lydstep Headland

I start with the visible and am startled by the visible – Dannie Abse

This balmy evening on the Headland
it is enough to be startled by the visible:
behind me six Welsh Blacks snuffling at what grass
they can find between the clumps of gorse.

An August moon three-quarters silver
set above the south horizon that is rusty-rose,
magenta and grey in layers
holding the charcoal smudge of Lundy Island.

The Headland's sloping cliff edge falls sheer from my feet.
This is where I scattered my father.
The sea is a wide, flat lake stirred only by currents
and the surface creases of a fitful breeze.

Then one, two, three birds
rise from nothing –
black-backed gulls that soar and dip
for fish only they can see.

I know that Somerset and Devon,
lights and lives, are over the southern edge;
and to the west sailing for days
nothing until America.

In the fragile focus of my field glasses
that tightening O-O of sharpened vision,
the black tipped span of the gull becomes immense:
my Pembrokeshire albatross.

A scattering

Four months to the day she died I walk on to the Headland
through the dark woods where it is muddy
and the cattle stand tired and sullen after days of rain.

Then along the path to the wide sky,
the rain having cleared the air,
bringing the colours of the cliffs and fields alive.

A smooth ebb tide in the Haven where the lights are coming on
and the gulls settling on the column of rock
at the mouth of the old limestone quarry below.

I move more slowly to the teetering edge of the Point
to face the end of the islands,
the last yellow of Sandtop Bay.

This is as far as your father and mother went with her ashes,
Madeleine plump with you and Gareth,
our big, muscled surfer, all passion and sadness,

standing on the very edge where I could not go
to shake his grandmother into the wind
over the limestone drop to the green sea.

This evening's held a quiet and lonely moment.
A kestrel rises from the cliff's face
and startles me. I shout twice *Huw Arthur!* over the sea;

too many memories and not a prayer.
Then your name – *Huw Arthur* –
once more, as a whisper.

St Elidyr's, Amroth

Six men straining to carry you to rest, Jim,
on a day when the trees are heavy with December mist
and the vicar's words are beaten down
by the weather and the sea.

All born on Earth must die. Destruction reigns
Round the whole globe and changes all its scenes

Then the sprinkling of fine soil on your lid
and the glint of sliced earth ready under its faux-grass cloth.
So cold. With the solstice tide
beating like a heart – shush, shush, from the grey beyond.

Time brushes off our lives with sweeping wing
And to the graves our earthly tents doth bring

Saint Elidyr invited underground by the little folk
played their games and lived on saffron milk
until his greed for their gold brought him back
to the everyday world. Then to Christ. Then repentance.

Where they shall lie till Christ's reviving day
When glorious souls shall wear refined clay

Lives such as ours journey down to this: no further.
Rooted to the coast, our people, farmers, miners, being
land-bound, though close to the sea. Saint Elidyr
breaking open the earth to find nothing.

Amroth in October

This afternoon we've come to see your new stone,
Jim, and place some flowers and pause a while.
The grass is full of last night's rain
and so much warmer than your last December day.

They've diverted us through that muddy lane
that winds up past the farm: logging in progress.
The sea's drowned out by chainsaws
and the crashing of the pines on that slope –
dangerous work, the sort your old man
would have relished taking on.
But Jeanette and the girls and visitors such as we
will have a clear view of the bay next time.

We're in the Semis tomorrow, Jim,
and the whole country's up for it,
full of hope, running out on the field of praise again.
Though the young fly-half's shoulder's gone and Hook is in:
you'll be turning in this grave over that.

What was it you were saying the final time we met,
last autumn's international – the All Blacks,
watched together in your front room?
"Hook's a prancer"? "Fancy dancer"? "Prat"?
That match stirred the last of your embers.

We front row toilers were always envious of those boys.
But now you're packed down again
and "the 'ooker from Carmarthen" is here today
between your shoulder and A.N.Other's fresh clay.

Your headstone's a classy marble with a waved top
like your fifteen-year old's quiff in our school team photo,
or Gerald's curvy running and swing of the hip
(I jink, therefore I am)
ghosting past a man off his educated left peg.

It's the French on Saturday
and we have the beating of them:
just as you must have felt that afternoon in '64
at the old Arms Park, your only Schools cap –
v. France, the *French Scholaires*.
A dull slog of a match that could have done
with a flashy fly-half dancer –
Phil Bennett, Cliff Morgan, King John.

From the stands we thought you'd held your own,
but that was to be your one and only chance,
like Denzil Thomas (Neath, Llanelly, Wales)
who taught us, that chunky centre three-quarter
– a match-winning one cap wonder.

It's been the best part of a year:
you've missed the Six Nations,
most of this World Cup – England going out,
our steady progress, because, we're sure,
this one has our name on it.

Missing too the rich smell of the cut pines and smoke
drifting across from that hill today, and at Manorbier
our first ever pair of Red Kites seen high and clear
this morning on the coastal path from Swanlake Bay.
To fix this small pot of cyclamen we have brought
I plant my heel and make a mark in your clay.

Wanting Choughs

The last living thing
to be seen by Mallory in '24
as the mountain squeezed his breath away
was surely a chough,
for they are recorded near the summit
by Norton and, who knows, in '53
may well have been drawn to the biscuits
hurriedly buried by Tensing Norgay,
his Buddhist offering to Everest,
as he and Hillary paused at the peak
for as long as their oxygen would allow.

Those perpetually moving beaks,
Coronation flunkies in the Himalayan abbey,
their bright legs like Elizabethan courtiers,
as Noyce saw them, choughs drawn
to the droppings of the climbers,
their tea-leaves, the spillage of their camp.

A chough: that would be a thing indeed,
that would make my year;
but each time I walk our Headland
they are nowhere to be seen.
Reported by others, a certain pair
at least, clear against Whitesheet Rock,
but the constant crosses of black
against blue and green
are always for me no more than
the common *Corvus*, crow or raven,
never the red-beaked, red legged
undisputed primal, heraldic chough.

I've seen them on the island of Skomer,
common enough and close enough
to linger in the lens, strut their flashy stuff –
polished boot-black wings and legs full-gaitered.
But here at Lydstep,

where we scattered my father and mother,
nothing.
        There's bullying black-backed gulls, rock pigeons,
once a peregrine's feeding stoop,
launched from its nest scrape in the cliffs,
hunting between Smuggler's Cave and Mother Carey's Kitchen,
but the choughs of Everest and Skomer and elsewhere
are a shape in the mind and not the evening air.

Though I should want them often to appear
for friends and family
and those who never knew me
or ever read a word of mine,
but come to the Headland for the sea's green heartbeat
and a sky that goes on forever,
if my ashes were emptied out here.

Dylan at One Hundred

This year's winding down past another November
from your hundredth beginning marked with fanfare,
fuss and stir: celebrations
of your words and your small legends
of hurt and disgrace, actual, imagined,
or remembered larger than they were.

It seems that after the first death
there are still scenes to play out,
so that your short life, shambling and shrill,
thrusts out of a Laugharne dug–deep skull
like a stubborn, willed flowering, a shout
from that blind mouth and every dumb socket's breath.

Dilly, dilly, the heron stabs at the tide, still
the sun is caged by Sir John's Hill,
and the captains of your fate, blind, knowing,
rake over the leaves of your scribbling.
Better we should read the stories as stories, hear
the poems performed, yours and Yeats, Hardy, de la Mare:

and listen (not watch) to conjure *Under Milk Wood*.
The loud boys and the knowing girls are all gone under,
the Chelsea Hotel's apartments now, the White Horse clear of smoke.
And though a new century's singing has stolen your thunder
we still lean into every weathered word you spoke.
(Take a pinch of the bad and swallow the good.)

Your country churchyard bare bones' sleep goes on,
your wordy dreams take flight with each heron and hawk's lift
whether the grave visitors catch their drift
or not. Characters hammer their heads up through every page
and voices, theirs, yours, are constantly re-born:
opening the book lets you strut your stage.

Birthday Poem for Dannie Abse at Ninety

im. Dannie (1923-2014)

Oh, write and paint and play, old men, and never count the cost,
the road is long and lonely
and the indifferent gods are lost.

In his ninetieth year to heaven
an artist may still stroke the canvas with a broad brush,
still cut precise lines in the plate
so flounce of hair and target of nipple
are there from memory, still there.

Oh, fuck me, famed Picasso, treat me harsh and kind:
Time's Fool rides a wilful steed
and the bearded gods are blind.

The burin's stipple, the cutting groove
of his graver dissects and reveals the world
still fresh. The carnival processes,
the faces press from the edge of things
to witness how past and present move.

Old lover, Monsieur Degas sees you take me from behind:
Time's voyeur rides a comely steed
when the bearded gods are blind.

The chevallier's posed for a portrait: he's tricked,
his green cocked hat perched like a bird;
his braid and medals shining, chivalric –
Mosquetero con espada
his sword clutched like a crucifix.

Oh, fight me, Pablo Ruiz, cross swords just one more time,
for life is in the balance
and the indifferent gods are blind.

La *Banista*'s in the ocean again, far from the beach;
the waves transport her, divide limbs from breasts
then re-construct her as one green movement,
a lyric of water. She points or strokes
to a horizon she must reach.

Oh, save me, Senor Pablo, I'm drifting in the wind:
Time's Fool risks a rising tide
and the salt-beard Gods unkind.

This *Mujer* kisses so sweetly the beak
of a small, blue bird she holds up to her face.
Her eyes have slipped from their proper place,
her hat, her hair, her head are become bird
and she cannot speak.

Oh, paint me, my Old Master, with brush strokes soft and kind:
your blues can bring me back to life
for the worn-out gods are blind.

The heart of great Matisse gave out
in his ninth decade, leaving Vence the finest chapel
ever completed by an atheist. Then his cut
paper was collaged into a splintered snail
that turned a world of colours and shapes.

Oh, bless the world with colour though your beard is white, Henri;
through the shuttered window, past the patterned walls
the boats are asleep on an endless summer sea.

Dave Brubeck, the master who in five/four conquered time,
in his ninth decade still played, composed and worked:
he'd walk so slowly, stiffly to the Steinway
but at the keys the years dropped off as he began to play
Unsquare Dance, Take Five, Blue Rondo a la Turk.

So play for us, old masters, play fast and out of time:
your fingers kiss the ivory
and breathe the world alive.

We are the sum of all we've heard and seen and drawn.
Old Welsh parrot, Dannie, sing once more for us –
speak honestly and true of Iolo, Leo, Joan,
the lines you have rehearsed so long,
the lovely lies we need from you.

Oh, paint and write and play, old men, and never count the cost,
the road is long and lonely
and the indifferent gods are lost.

A Pembrokeshire Artist

John Knapp Fisher (1931 -2015)

An evening with the rain coming in,
that sea so cold and unsettled, a heavy graphite,
you'd not have gone out with your mackerel lines
in the Viking or any of her successors
from the stone-brick embrace of Porthgain.

We've eaten our fill at your wake, John,
the Sloop Inn squeezed tight
with suits, black ties and memories.
Wives, patrons, grandchildren.
Photos of you through all seven ages on the screen.

Inland to Wolf's Castle and as far south as the cathedral
the farms, haggards and holiday lets
shrug down for the cold night.
You'd have worked to conjure the reluctant light
discovered in them under this empting, moonless sky.

And the first scurp coming would have dabbed
your paper, blossomed and been coaxed,
smudged, into the finished sketch.
Now the county will have to sing its own spirit,
compose its own shape, keep its own watch.

Workshop

Poetry is that
which comes at the heart
by way of the intellect.

And this is the place where
(who knows?) one of us
might struggle or stumble

into or across a poem
and carry the music of it through our lives
like a poppy picked out of a wide field of corn,

the green island squeezed into being between sea and sky,
that electric metal flash from the spine of a mackerel,
like a rhyme ringing out of the commonwealth of prose.

Seamus on the Tube

Looking away, not looking away –
The happenstance of what may change everything;
Those standing commuters moving off at Charing Cross
For the Bakerloo Line and then your eyes lifting

Above those seated opposite, as one does, to read
Between faster Broadband and Las Vegas –
"Where your accent is an aphrodisiac," it says,
And where "what happens here, stays here,"

The Railway Children where in the white cups
Of the telegraph wires a young boy knows
That words are carried in the shiny pouches of raindrops.
Like this poem carried for you in the red and white Tube

On the Northern Line in cold January's real freeze;
Snow is promised in the suburbs so everyone's scarved
Against the weather. Words taking you back to the fifties
And his boyhood summers before everything changed.

Reaching Warren Street, you've read it
Four or five times, absorbed the innocent wisdom
And sense of the thing. Those people opposite
See a crazy old man mouthing words, appearing to sing.